SS-Freiwilligen-Grenadier-Division "Nordland"

The 11th SS-Freiwilligen-Grenadier-Division "Nordland"

Rolf Michaelis

Schiffer Military History
Atglen, PA

Book translation by Dr. Edward Force.

Book Design by Ian Robertson.

Library of Congress Control Number: 2008938127

Printed in China.
ISBN: 978-0-7643-3100-8

This book was originally published in German under the title
Die 11. SS-Freiwilligen-Grenadier-Division "Nordland" by Michaelis-Verlag

We are interested in hearing from authors with book ideas on related topics.

Published by Schiffer Publishing Ltd.
4880 Lower Valley Road
Atglen, PA 19310
Phone: (610) 593-1777
FAX: (610) 593-2002
E-mail: Info@schifferbooks.com.
Visit our web site at: www.schifferbooks.com
Please write for a free catalog.
This book may be purchased from the publisher.
Please include $5.00 postage.
Try your bookstore first.

In Europe, Schiffer books are distributed by:
Bushwood Books
6 Marksbury Avenue
Kew Gardens
Surrey TW9 4JF, England
Phone: 44 (0) 20 8392-8585
FAX: 44 (0) 20 8392-9876
E-mail: Info@bushwoodbooks.co.uk.
Visit our website at: www.bushwoodbooks.co.uk
Free postage in the UK. Europe: air mail at cost.
Try your bookstore first.

Contents

Foreword

On the night of May 1, 1945, various groups of German soldiers and civilians tried to break out of encircled Berlin. Among the people who tried to cross the Weidendammer Bridge from the Friedrichstrasse Depot were the last survivors of the 11th *SS* Volunteer Armored Grenadier Division "Nordland". Up to this point, this *SS* unit had covered a course of some 5000 kilometers across Europe and had always fought at the focal points. Some 16,000 soldiers from the ranks of the division had fallen, been wounded, or gone missing.

This book is an attempt to recount the history of this formation. The situation of the *Waffen-SS* in 1943 (replacements, legions, and future planning), and the battles and combat of the group, originally called the "Germanic *SS* Armored Grenadier Division," will be emphasized.

The purpose of this work is to make a contribution to the historical view of the *Waffen-SS*. Along with the data from the Federal and Military Archives in Freiburg, numerous former native or ethnic Germans, as well as Scandinavian members and military historians, have helped me. To represent all of them, my thanks go to Hans Erlewein and Heinz Genzow, who not only encouraged me, but supported me in word and deed.

Berlin, October 2001
Rolf Michaelis

Forerunners of the Division

The Free Corps "Denmark"

With the beginning of the German Russian campaign on June 22, 1941, talks began between Germany and Denmark, which had been "occupied by German troops for its own protection" since 1940.The contents of these exchanges of views included the participation of Danish soldiers in the fight against the Soviet Union. The official sending of a strengthened regiment of the Danish Army was rejected by Denmark, for it saw its neutrality threatened. But since numerous Danes were ready to fight against Communism, and Germany, for reasons of propaganda, was interested in Danish participation in the war, they agreed on a "Denmark" volunteer band within the German Army.

Himmler's immediate interest in taking these volunteers into the *Waffen-SS* and integrating them into the *SS*-Standard "Nordland" of the *SS* "Wiking" Division was opposed by the German ambassador to Denmark, Renthe-Fink, who feared that scarcely any Danes would volunteer. Many of the potential volunteers had already—mostly as construction soldiers—fought on the Finnish side in the Finnish-Soviet Winter War of 1940-41, but had no great interest in National Socialism. They had first volunteered to the Finnish military command, but were rejected by the Finnish Army on the grounds of lacking possibilities. The *Reichsführer-SS* could at least arrange that the *SS* command office could take over the organizational direction. The *Wehrmacht* command agreed to that, since they were under no pressure, but the "Denmark" volunteer unit remained under their command. The leader of the Danish National Socialist Worker Party (DNSAP), Fritz Clausen, advocated that members of his party join the volunteer unit, and not a few men of his *Storm Afedlingen* (SA) volunteered. As opposed to the *SS* Standard "Nordland," formed on April 20, 1940, the volunteer unit was to be a purely Danish one. Thus, the language problem, not to be underestimated, was eliminated in the lower ranks. While the Germanic-National Socialistic concept was to prevail in the *SS* "Nordland" Standard (*SS* "Wiking" Division), setting this goal was shared in the volunteer unit. Here many also served who just wanted to fight against Bolshevism but had no National Socialist goals. The *SS* was aware of this, and thus one could read the following propaganda text in an *SS* guidebook:[1]

1. SS-Leitheft, Year 7, Issue 7b.

"In the legions there thus dominates—with all relationship of the will to fight and the Germanic manner—a very active picture. The picture becomes different, though, when we turn to that formation of the Waffen-SS *in which it is undertaken to develop the unity of the Germanic peoples, present in their blood, with a bold grip but yet in systematic educational manner.—That is the* Wiking *Division."*

There were also numerous ethnic German volunteers from North Schleswig,[2] which had passed to Denmark on July 5, 1920. The Danish side suggested Lt. Col. Christian-Peter Kryssing[3] as the group's commander, and as of July 1, 1941, he was installed as the Legion's *Obersturmbannführer*. The Danish media announced the establishment of the "Daenemark" volunteer unit on July 3, 1941, and the Danish defense minister proclaimed on July 8, 1941, that the Danish government had no objection to active or discharged soldiers voluntarily reporting for armed service. Accordingly, all were allowed to volunteer who had finished their military service since 1931. Hitler's establishment order followed on July 15, 1941.[4] Just four days later, 480 Danish volunteers were retired in Copenhagen in the presence of the Chief of the *SS Gruppenführer's* headquarters and Lieutenant General Berger of the *Waffen-SS*.

Housed at first in the *SS* barracks at Hamburg-Langenhorn and strengthened by some 100 Danes of the *SS* Volunteer *Standarte* "Nordwest," the volunteers were sworn in on August 5, 1941. On August 15, 1941, the unit was designated "Free Corps[5] Danmark"[6] and was transferred to Posen-Treskau on September 13, 1941, for further training.[7] In the course of the next few weeks the opposing viewpoints within the Free Corps came to light. Kryssing, along with his ethnic German adjutant Lorenzen of North Schleswig, took one side, and did not want to allow any National Socialist propaganda in their unit. Great portions of the officer corps and about half of the men who had come from the ranks of the NSDAP—some via the *SS* "Nordland" Standard—took the other side. The situation escalated when Kryssing had a young Dane arrested because of NS propaganda

2. After a plebiscite in February 1920, North Schleswig was given to Denmark. 75,431 (74.2%) of the inhabitants had voted for Denmark and only 25,329 (24.9%) for Germany. On 4 March of that year, the vote was cast in South Schleswig. There 51,392 (80%) of the voters voted for Germany and only 12,924 (20%) for Denmark. Thus, South Schleswig remained within the German boundary.

3. See Appendix 9.

4. Command to establish a "Daenemark" volunteer unit, *SS*-FHA *Abt. Org. Tgb.* 2780/41 of July 12, 1941.

5. The designation of "Free Corps" was used because Denmark was occupied by German troops in April 1940 "*only to protect its neutrality*" without opposition (sic!). The Danish Army was not disbanded as a potential source of danger until the summer of 1943. In the countries that were—more or less—conquered in battle, "Volunteer Legions" were established.

6. Command Sheet of the *Waffen-SS* of August 15, 1941, No. 316.

and alleged calls for mutiny. After graffiti such as, for example, "Away with the Democrat Kryssing" were to be read in the barracks area, the *SS* Command Headquarters intervened. On February 13, 1942, *SS Gruppenführer* and Lieutenant General of the *Waffen-SS* Walter Krüger[8] arrived at Potsdam-Treskau and investigated the events. Ten days later, Legion *Obersturmbannführer* Kryssing and *SS-Untersturmbannführer* Lorenzen were removed from their positions and transferred to the *Führer* Reserve of the *SS*-FHA. Their successor was the Danish National Socialist *SS-Sturmbannführer* Frederik von Schalburg, who had served until then in the *SS* "Wiking" Division.

At the end of April 1942, the Free Corps, with a strength of some 800 men, received the order to take part in the upcoming combat action; a few days later, they marched to the eastern front. There the Red Army had been able on January 8, 1942, to surround the II. Army Corps near Demyansk. The "Danmark" Free Corps arrived first at Heiligenbeil, near Koenigsberg, and was transported by air from there to Demyansk. Subordinated to the *SS Totenkopf* Division, the Danes took up positions on the Lovat on May 20, 1942. On June 2, 1942, *SS Sturmbannführer* von Schalburg fell in action. *SS Obersturmbannführer* von Lettow-Vorbeck took command.

Three days later, parts of the *SS Totenkopf* Division, along with the Free Corps, led Operation "Danebrog"—the attack on the strategic focal point of Bolshoye Dubovizy, on the Pola—in a pouring rain. Sometimes standing in a swamp up to their hips, the Danes were able to occupy the town on June 11, 1942, after back-and-forth combat, and capture numerous heavy and light weapons. When *SS Obersturmbannführer* von Lettow-Vorbeck fell on that day, Legion *Hauptsturmbannführer* Martinsen took command. Six days later the Soviet troops began a major attack in the area of the Danish volunteers and the neighboring Jäger Regiment 28 (Colonel Roericht) of the 8th Jäger Division. When the Free Corps was withdrawn from the front on June 26, 1942, it had lost nine officers and 337 other ranks in the fighting. The Commanding General of the II. Army Corps, General of the Infantry Graf von Brockdorff-Ahlefeldt,[9] released the Danes on August 1, 1942:

"*Since the 8th of May, the 'Danmark' Legion has been positioned in the fortress* [of Demyansk, author's note]. *True to your oath and mindful of the heroic death of your first commander,* SS Sturmbannführer *von Sxchalburg, you, the officers and men of the Legion, have always given renewed proof of the greatest bravery and readiness to make sacrifices, as well as signs of exemplary toughness and endurance.*

8. See Appendix 9.
9. See Appendix 9.

"The comrades of the Army and the Waffen-SS *are proud of being able to fight shoulder to shoulder with you in the truest armed brotherhood. I thank you for your loyalty and bravery."*

On August 9, 1942, the "Danmark" Free Corps reached Russa Telebya viz Staraya and went from there by rail via Pleskau-Riga to Mitau. On September 7, 1942, the Danes received a four-week furlough. The propaganda success wanted by the German side was not gained; on the contrary, the provocative appearance of numerous Free Corps members—especially of the NSDAP—led to tensions with the population. The Free Corps had practically no link with their own country except the DNSAP, and the party in turn had no link with the Danish people. On October 18, 1942, the volunteers arrived back in Mitau.

On November 21, 1942, the "Danmark" Free Corps was transferred to Bobruisk. The replacement company also followed it from Posen-Treskau. On December 1, 1942, Himmler subordinated the Free Corps to the 1st *SS* Infantry Brigade 9 (mot.),[10] and it in turn to the OKH directly for front service at Velikiye Luki. Under the command of Legion

The action of the "Danmark" Free Corps in the Demyansk pocket, May 3-July 26, 1942.

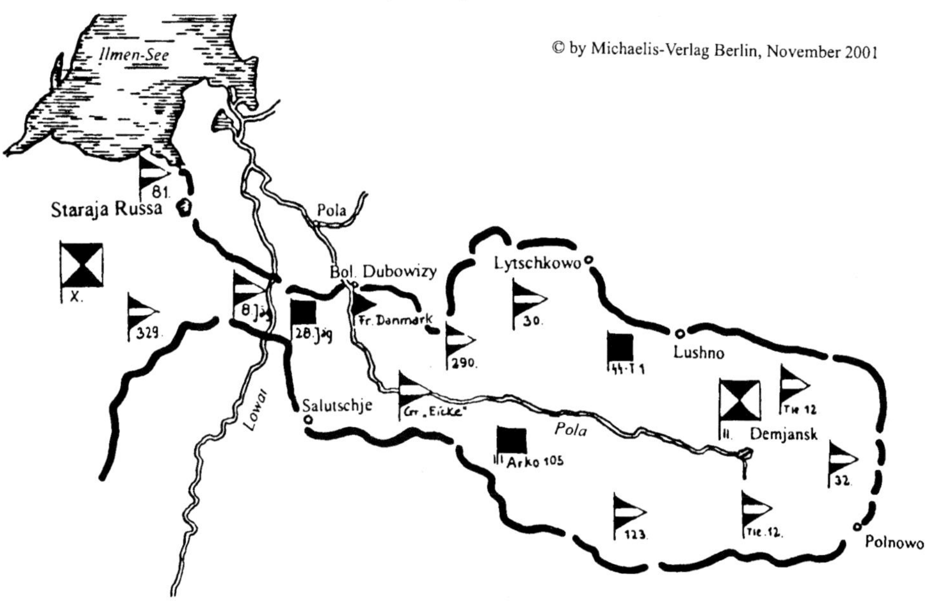

10. The 1st *SS* Infantry Brigade (mot.) was formed on April 24, 1941,and subordinated on June 21, 1941, to the Command Staff of "*Reichsführer-SS*" for action in the backline area. Along with fighting scattered Soviet troops in the process of the fast German advance, parts of the brigade shot hundreds of Jews and Gypsies frequently until the autumn of 1941.

Sturmbannführer Martinsen, the 1100 Danes marched to Nevel the next day, reaching it on December 5, 1942. Here, on the line between Army Groups North and Center, the Soviet 3rd Assault Army under Lieutenant General Purkayev had succeeded in surrounding parts of the 83rd Infantry Division at Velikiye Luki, northeast of Nevel, on November 19-20, 1942.

After the Free Corps had assembled near Girlovo on December 9, 1942, the Danes held the HKL at Poretchye until December 15, 1942, south of the German "Wöhler" Relief Group. Then the unit was transferred to the area between Klevniki, on the Lovat, and Kandratovo, on the Balasdyn. At the end of December 1942 the "Danmark" Free Corps, with a strength of only 12 officers and 630 other ranks, took positions along the Ushyza to the Usho Lake.

Action of the "Danmark" Free Corps (December 1942 to March 1943)

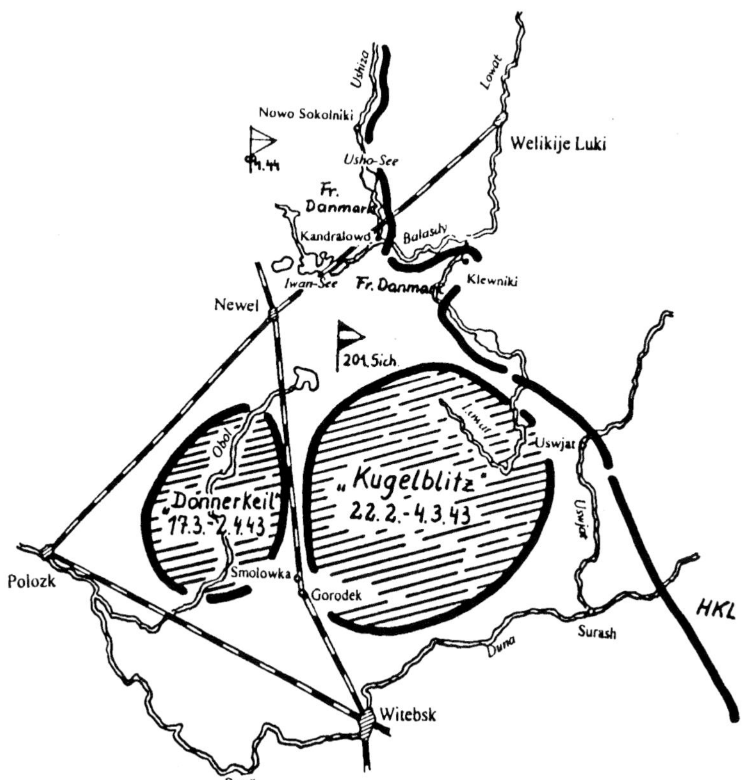

After Soviet counterattacks, the brigade went into front action near Orel early in December 1941. From August 11 to December 1, 1942, it fought against partisans in the greater Minsk area. Then the 1st *SS* Infantry Brigade (mot.) was subordinated to the OKH for new front action.

At the beginning of February 1943, Legion *Sturmbannführer* Martinsen turned the Free Corps over to Legion *Hauptsturmführer* Neergard-Jacobsen and formed the Schalburg Corps in Denmark. This corps, at first intended to be a replacement unit for the Free Corps, developed into a political police unit that was used by the German Reich against sabotage and political action by Danes in their own country.

As of February 22, 1943, the "Danmark" Free Corps took part in Operation "Kugelblitz" under the central command of the 3rd Panzer Army. Partisans in the wooded area north of Surash, some of whom had moved toward the front near Usvyat, were to be put down. There were six brigades in action breaking the Vitebsk-Nevel transit line, especially in the Gorodok-Smolovka area, which made German administration and operations in that region almost impossible, and carrying out numerous actions in the westward areas of the Reich Commissariat "Ostland." The danger caused by the nearby front was also undeniable. Seeing action were:

- 201st Security Division (Major General Jacobi[11]) with
    - Security Regiment 601
    - Bicycle Security Regiment 2
    - Free Corps "Danmark"
    - Parts of Flying Regiment 23[12]
- Commander of the Eastern Troops z.b.V. 703 (Major General von Wartenberg[13])
    - Cossack Battalion 622
    - Cossack Battalion 623
    - Cossack Battalion 631
    - One battalion of Volga Tatars

The operation was made difficult from the beginning by the mining of the only roads in the lake district and the destruction of the bridges. Overrun by the Volga Tatars on the first day of action, the barrage line in the Duena area could be secured only provisionally. During the next days the Volga Tatars saw action on the partisan side, and the Cossacks stood out as before for their ability and bravery.

The village of Krasny Dvor (17 km northwest of Vitebsk) and the wooded area on both sides of the lakes, especially the Koslovici Lake (37 km north of Vitebsk), turned out to be the partisans' main support points. The Secret Field Police and Action Command 9 of

11. See Appendix 9.

12. Flying Regiment 23 developed from Flight Training Regiment 23, and was transferred from Belfort to Russia in the autumn of 1942. It consisted of two battalions of five companies each, and was partly equipped with captured Russian weapons. Since the end of 1942, the regiment protected the railroad along the Vitebsk-Nevel line near Gorodok. The 1st Battalion held a bunker line to the south, while the 2nd Battalion held one to the north. Parts of the regiment took part in mobile partisan fighting in the spring of 1943.

13. See Appendix 9.

the SD examined 169 villages and 3583 people. Of them, 804 were sent to concentration camps, while 227 known partisans and 406 of their helpers were shot. Action Command 9 of the SD also reported the shooting of 823 known and suspected partisans (including 127 women, 33 Volga Tatar deserters, and four Jews).

In the final report on the operation, which concluded on March 4, 1943, the 201st Security Division recorded a total of 3738 dead and 260 captured partisans. The losses of the German forces were 117 dead, 334 wounded, and 21 missing.

On March 17, 1943, the 3rd Panzer Army was already planning Operation "Donnerkeil." In it, the 201st Security Division was to smash the "Fililayev," "Markov," "Romanov," and "Koretkin" partisan brigades, as well as the partisans in the Mossoyova-Trudy swamp area, who had retreated over the Vitebsk-Nevel line during Operation "Kugelblitz." Along with four battalions of the Commander of the Eastern Troops,[14] the "Danmark" Free Corps took part in the fighting again. Although the combat conditions were considerably less favorable (the soldiers sometimes had to wade in mud up to their hips), the attack goals could almost always be achieved. But when the operation was halted on April 2, 1943, it was seen again that most of the partisans had avoided the encircling ring.

The Danish volunteers were taken out of action and ordered to the Grafenwöhr troop training camp. The replacement company arrived there from Bobruisk on May 1, 1943. Effective May 20, 1943, the strong Free Corps was disbanded and transferred into the newly established *SS* Volunteer Armored Grenadier Regiment "Danmark."

14. The Cossack Battalions 622 and 623, under the command of the later Knight's Cross bearer, Major Ewert von Renteln, stood out particularly there.

The Volunteer Legion "Norwegen"

After German troops had occupied Norway in April 1940, Himmler tried to recruit Norwegian National Socialists to fight for the "*Great German Reich*." His success was meager: in 18 months, only 291 volunteers registered to join the *SS Standarte* "Nordland." After the Russian campaign began, many more Norwegians were ready to serve in the Finnish Army. The unreal plans of Vidkun Quisling, the *Führer* of the right-leaning *Nasjonal Samling*, to set up a 30,000-man volunteer corps for the eastern front were no longer considered by Hitler. But on June 29, 1941, he approved a gathering of Norwegian volunteers in a legion to fight against Bolshevism.

The German *Reich* Commissar for Norway announced this grandly in a radio broadcast, and the *SS* Command organized the formation as of August 1, 1941. Trained at the Fallingbostel camp (Bergen/Celle), the Norwegian volunteers were sworn in on October 3, 1941, in the presence of the Chief of the *SS* Command Headquarters, *SS Gruppenführer* and Lieutenant General of the *Waffen-SS* Jüttner. Effective January 15, 1942, a replacement company was set up at Holmestrand, near Oslo.

When the Volunteer Legion "Norwegen" was ordered from Fallingbostel to the front near Leningrad at the end of February 1942, 1218 Norwegians had volunteered. On March 16, 1942, the troops reached the area of the L. Army Corps and were subordinated to the Police Battle Group "Jeckeln" on the boundary of the XXVI. Army Corps north of Krasnoye Selo, near Urizk-Stara Panovo. The battle group, under the command of the Higher *SS* and Police *Führer* Russia-North *SS Gruppenführer* and Lieutenant General of the Police Jeckeln, had recently taken over the sector of the 58th Infantry Division from the coast to and including Pushkin, and thus consisted of:

- Infantry Regiment 320 (212th Infantry Division) with subordinated
    - Police Battalion 306
    - Police Battalion 212
- Staff Infantry Regiment 409 (122nd Infantry Division) with
    - Reconnaissance Battalion 158 (58th Infantry Division)
    - V. SS "Leibstandarte Adolf Hitler"
    - Police Battalion 56
    - Police Battalion 310
    - Volunteer Legion "Norwegen"
    - Police Battalion 305
- Parts of heavy units (*Panzerjäger*, infantry guns, and artillery) of the 58th Infantry and *SS* Police Divisions.

In mid-May 1942 the Volunteer Legion "Norwegen" was released from the III./Infantry Regiment 538 (385th Infantry Division) and, after several days' rest, took over the area of the II./Infantry Regiment 538 before Pulkovo.

On August 13, 1942, the "Jeckeln" Police Battle Group was disbanded. The "Norwegen" Volunteer Legion remained in the area and was still subordinated to the L. Army Corps. Their neighbor to the right in the XXVI. Army Corps was then the 227th Infantry Division. Even before the German Operation "Nordlicht," in which Leningrad was supposed to be taken on September 14, 1942, the Red Army began its own offensive on August 24, 1942. The goal of the Soviet Leningrad and Volkov front was to establish a land connection with Leningrad and wipe out the German 11th Army, which was marching up from Crimea. The main thrust struck the XXVI. Army Corps and also caused heavy losses to neighboring units, including the "Norwegen" Volunteer Legion.

The enemy troops were able to build up their breakthrough on September 3, 1942, but then lost their attacking impetus. Here the commander of the 11th Army, Field Marshal Manstein,[15] moved in and was able to cut off the Soviet units near Tortolovo from their backline connections. As before in the Volkov pocket, the surrounded enemy forces were crushed. By the end of the month the Red Army lost seven divisions and six brigades.

On October 8, 1942, the L. Army Corps was composed of:

- 2. *SS* Infantry Brigade (mot.)
- Parts of the 58th Infantry Division
- 225th Infantry Division
- 215th Infantry Division
- 1/3 of the 385th Infantry Division
- "Norwegen" Volunteer Legion

At the end of November 1942, the "Norwegen" Volunteer Legion was subordinated to the command of the 2nd *SS* Infantry Brigade (mot.),[16] which likewise belonged to the L. Army Group since the end of August 1942. After the Soviet command transferred the focal points of their operations to the southern sector of the eastern front, numerous German troops were transferred away from the Army Group North. Taking Leningrad had thus become impossible. By 1944 only a siege ring remained around the city.

---

15. See Appendix 9.
16. The 2nd *SS* Infantry Brigade (mot.) was formed on April 24, 1941, and subordinated to the "Reichsführer SS" command staff on June 21, 1941, for action in the backland area. In the process of Soviet counterattacks, the brigade moved into front action before Leningrad in the autumn of 1941. When the *SS* Infantry Regiment 4 (mot.) was taken out of the brigade's zone in 1942, the unit gained three Latvian police battalions. In May 1943 the brigade reached the Volkov. Here the *SS* Infantry Regiment 14 (mot.) was also replaced by three Latvian police battalions, and the unit was renamed the Latvian *SS* Volunteers.

On December 31, 1942, the "Norwegen" Volunteer Legion had a strength of only 20 leaders and 678 other ranks. While the second battle of Ladoga was begun by the Soviet 2nd Assault Army (Lt. Gen. Romanovsky) in January 1943, the Legion was still on the right wing of the L. Army Corps. Its right-hand neighbor in the LIV. Army Corps was the 250th (Spanish) Infantry Division. Until the end of February 1943, the Norwegians had the hardest battles to come through. Then they were removed from the front and ordered to the Mitau area. From there the circa 600 surviving Norwegian volunteers reached the Grafenwöhr training camp in March 1943, and the Legion was disbanded there on May 20, 1943. The volunteers finally acted as a cadre for the newly founded *SS* Volunteer Armored Grenadier Regiment "Norge." John Sandstad was a member of the "Norwegen" Volunteer Legion:

"I was born on February 5, 1925, in Hunan, China, the son of a Norwegian missionary. In 1932 my father had to leave China for health reasons, and he bought a small farm in Norway. Since I saw a serious danger for the Nordic lands and Western Europe after the

The Action Area of the "Norwegen" Volunteer Legion
(March 1942 to March 1943)

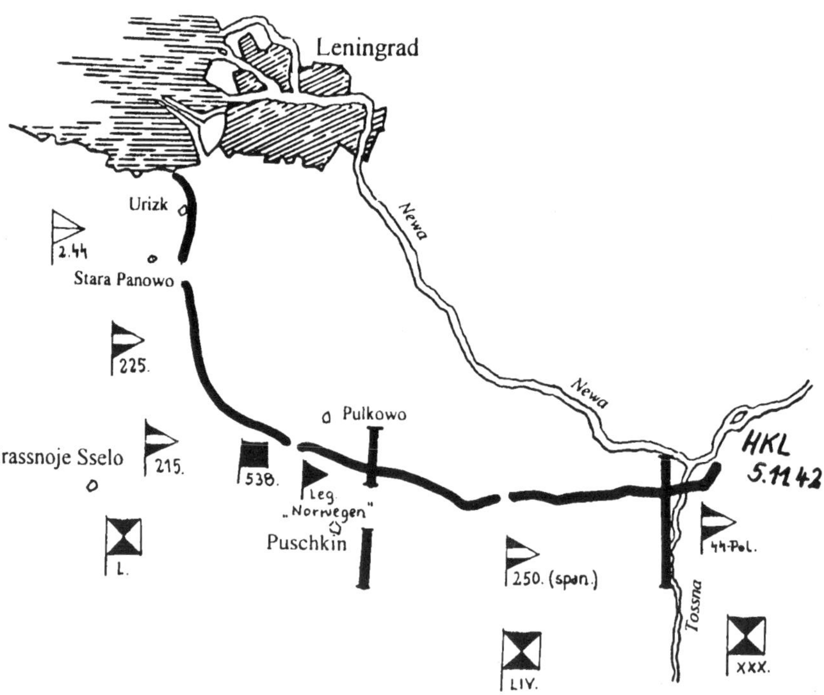

Soviet attack on Finland in 1939-40, I volunteered for the 'Norwegen' Volunteer Legion in 1942. Shortly before that two of my friends had volunteered, and had been taken after one or two weeks. My call followed only after six weeks, which annoyed me very much, since I was not in the same company with them.

In the Replacement Command of the Waffen-SS *in Norway (Oslo) I was examined, and then I traveled with two boys from eastern Norway to Holmestrand, southwest of Oslo. On July 10, 1942, my service began at the training camp of the legion replacement. There was a half-trained rifle company there, plus a heavy company being formed, to which I went. At first there were only 20 to 30 of us, but some new men came every week. Early in August 1942 the rifle company was transferred to the Leningrad front.*

Our heavy company of about 80 men reached Mitau (Jelgava), Latvia, early in October 1942. Here we were housed in a former hunting lodge or estate about two kilometers outside the city. A few new men joined us there. The training was tough, the instructors were German, and so was the language of command. In general, the relationship between the German instructors and us was good—only our platoon leader, an SS Oberscharführer, *was somewhat moody, which we began to suspect.*

When we were ready for action in January 1943, the 'Norwegen' Volunteer Legion was withdrawn from front service a short time later. Our company was thus a replacement unit without a front unit. While some of us went to Dresden (engineers) or Holland (infantry guns) for special training, I and others became assistant instructors for new Norwegian volunteers.

On March 16, 1943, the Reichsführer-SS *visited us at Mitau. After inspection he gave a speech, in which he spoke of the future formation of the 'Norge' Regiment. We could also ask him questions later, in a relaxed atmosphere. One of us asked him where things stood on the so-called 'Jewish question.' Himmler answered us that negotiations were going on between Germany and France concerning Madagascar, to set up a Jewish state there.*[17] *Although he was not a soldier type—slimly built and wearing glasses—I found him very congenial then. At the end of March we were transferred to Grafenwöhr-Auerbach.*"

Ingebret Lilleborge was also in the "Norwegen" Volunteer Legion:

"*I was born in Borge-Fredrikstad in 1920 and volunteered—like most of us—for service in Finland. Our thoughts were that we wanted to help Finland and fight against the Communists. In August 1942 I was called up for the 1st Replacement Company of the*

17. This was deliberate disinformation from Himmler, for the Madagascar plan was only considered in 1940.

'Norwegen' Volunteer Legion. We went from Oslo to Stettin by ship, and then by train to Muelhausen. Then by truck to the Sennheim camp. There were big two-story buildings, which were also occupied by other units of the Waffen-SS *(Danes, Hollanders, etc.). All the recruits were chased around the area. Our company (about 130 men) had German instructors, who kept us busy all day from 6:00 on. There was also theoretical instruction in the halls. It was a hard life for us ex-civilians, but it made proper soldiers of us.*

From the SS *training camp at Sennheim we were sent to Mitau, but we did not see action, and in March 1943 we were sent to Grafenwöhr for the formation of the* SS *Volunteer Armored Grenadier Regiment 'Norge.'"*

New Formation of the *Waffen-SS* Early in 1943

At the end of 1942 the German command was in its most difficult crisis of the war to date. The already visible losses of personnel and materials in Stalingrad and Africa resulted in drastic gaps in the German armed forces. On December 18, 1942, the OKW's war diary stated:

"*...the* Führer *commands that* Reich *Minister Speer immediately withdraw 50,000 men from the commercial economy in three groups, and also exchanges 150,000 men of young strength from the commercial economy for older soldiers and releases 100,000 men irretrievably for the armament industry.*"

On the next day Hitler ordered the general draft of hitherto undrafted men liable for duty and, among other things, the establishment of two new *SS* divisions[18] in the area of the High Commander "West." On January 5, 1943, the OKW diary reported on the replacement status of these two *SS* units:

"*Once again the assurance of replacements for the formation of two new* SS *divisions approved by the* Führer *as of February 1, 1943, is commanded. For them, 27,000 men born in 1925 are to be gained by advertising in the RAD, 10,000 men from Action Rue 43 exchange, and 5000 ethnic Germans; if the last-named 15,000 are not gathered, the birth year of 1925 is to provide a significantly higher number. The* Reich *Work* Führer *is asked for cooperation in the drafting of men born in 1925.*

To protect men of this age if possible, the chief of Army Armament and Commander of the Replacement Army is being instructed to urge members of the early birth years (1924 and 23) to volunteer for the SS*; also kv-men, who were not formerly regarded as*

18. These were the 9th *SS* Armored Grenadier Division "Hohenstaufen" and the 10th *SS* Armored Grenadier Division "Frundsberg."

eligible for the SS, *are to be inducted. Finally, another 800 men who were released by the V.G.A.D.*[19] *in the fall are to be made available to the* SS."

Since volunteers had numbered only 10,000 men by the end of January 1943, and their numbers would presumably increase to only 20,000, the planned drafting of 20,000 members of the war-vital commercial economy in April and May had to be increased. On February 6, 1943, the KTB/OKW noted that the establishment of the two *SS* divisions would be completed as of June 1, 1943.

On February 14, 1943, the OKW informed the Army General Staff and the Chief of Army Equipping and Commander of the Replacement Army that Hitler had already ordered Himmler to set up three new divisions—of Croatian, Lithuanian, and Latvian peoples—by the beginning of June 1943. The divisions were to be:

11th Latvian *SS* Volunteer Division
12th Lithuanian *SS* Volunteer Division
13th Croatian *SS* Volunteer Division.

In discussions between the Completion Office of the *Waffen-SS* and the General Army Office, the contingent of 60,000 volunteers was approved. Because of infringements in the "recruiting of volunteers," there were disagreements among the *Wehrmacht* command, General Army Office, *SS* Completion Office, and other offices. The *SS* distanced itself from the matters being discussed. The *Reich* Work Service Leader made regulations to rule out further unallowable recruitment within the *Reich* Work Service. It became clear that expansion of the *Waffen-SS* strictly from volunteers led to ever-greater difficulties.[20]

The difficulty of setting up further *SS* units with German volunteers, and the thought of merging smaller troop units into larger formations, gave Himmler the idea at the beginning of March 1943 of forming a Germanic *SS* corps. In a memo he defined his plans for western and northern European volunteers for 1943.[21] Accordingly, the Germanic *SS* Corps was to consist of the *SS* "Wiking" and "Nordland" Divisions.

19. Reinforced Border Patrol Service.
20. KTB/OKW on February 24, 1943.
21. See Appendix 2.

The Establishment of the *SS* Volunteer Armored Grenadier Division "Nordland"

In the course of the general restructuring of German divisions from three to two (armored) grenadier regiments, Himmler ordered on March 18, 1943, that the *SS* Armored Grenadier Regiment "Nordland" be separated from the *SS* Armored Grenadier Division "Wiking" and used as the cadre of a new *SS* division.[22] The plans to establish the new *SS* Volunteer Division with the name of the former regiment, "Nordland," were changed again. At first, the formation of an *SS* Armored Division "Nordland" was planned, which was to be made up—like the second division of the new Germanic *SS* Corps—of the *SS* "Wiking" Armored Division, of:

two armored grenadier regiments
one light regiment
one armored regiment
one artillery regiment
and the usual division units.

On March 22, 1943, Hitler ordered the formation of the "Nordland" Division, interestingly already designated as the 14th (Germanic) *SS* **Armored Grenadier** Division "Nordland," at the Mielau troop training camp. At first,

- the "Norwegen" Volunteer Legion (ca. 600 men at Mitau),
- the "Niederlande" Volunteer Legion (then still with the 2nd (mot.) SS Infantry Brigade),
- the "Danmark" Free Corps (ca. 650 men with the 1st *SS* (mot.) Infantry Brigade),
- and the *SS* "Nordland" Armored Grenadier Regiment

were to be the cadre for the

- Advance Regiment "Norge,"
- *SS* Armored Grenadier Regiment "Nederland," and
- *SS* Armored Grenadier Regiment "Danmark."

The artillery and armored regiments and the other technical units were to be formed new of *Reich* and ethnic Germans.

In the documents of the *SS* command Office, the division was listed on April 10, 1943, as the:

22. *Reichsführer-SS*, Tgb. No. 24/43, of March 18, 1943.

SS **Armored Grenadier** Division 11[23] (Germanic)

And Grafenwöhr was listed as its new formation site. The Division Commander was to be *SS* Brigade Leader and Major General of the *Waffen-SS* von Scholz.[24]

Himmler's plans to set up another "Germanic" *SS* division were opposed by the Nazi leaders of the various countries.[25] The party leader of the Danish National Socialists, Dr. Clausen,[26] opposed further use of Danish volunteers. Gustav Meissner recalls:[27]

"... *Clausen had a strong mistrust of the policy followed by the* SS *in Denmark. He stated that the* SS *had said of him that, if he could present 500 Danish volunteers for service, he was guaranteed recognition for his party. He had then supplied a contingent of 800 volunteers, who had gone, after June 22, 1941, to the 'Danmark' Free Corps and the most varied other units of the* Waffen-SS... *Now the* SS *was trying to form a Germanic corps ... and had already sent* Obersturmbannführer *Martinsen (Commander of the Free Corps) to Denmark for that purpose. The members of this Germanic Corps were to be sworn in by the* Reichsführer-SS *and be subordinate to his instructions...*

This step, meanwhile carried out, ... had given the Danish National Socialists and Clausen the feeling that the volunteers from the ranks of the German NSAP would not be of use to their own party, but rather be finally withdrawn from the party. He sees this as a break of the promise that was made to him by the SS *in the spring of 1941....*"

To address the great dissatisfaction of the Danish volunteers, the Danish envoy in Berlin, Mohr, visited the volunteers at Grafenwöhr on July 28-29, 1943. Many of them wanted to be released on account of the meanwhile changed conditions in Denmark—they were fearful of their future and that of their members—and of their being taken into a regular *SS* unit. Mohr just instructed the soldiers to fight on against Bolshevism![28]

Similar arguments were also raised by Vidkun Quisling,[29] the *Führer* of the *Nasjonal Samlung* (NS) in Norway, on whose urging the *Reichsführer-SS* at that time even considered

23. The renumbering of the division from 14 to 11 resulted from the delays in the previously planned new formation of Latvian and Croatian *SS* volunteer divisions and the non-formation of a Lithuanian *SS* Volunteer Division.
24. See Appendix 9.
25. See Appendix 3.
26. See Appendix 9.
27. Meissner, Gustav, *Denmark under the Swastika*, Frankfurt am Main 1990.
28. It is noteworthy that the Danish postwar regime generally did not punish the action of volunteers in the "Danmark" Free Corps, while it regarded their service in the *Waffen-SS* as of August 1, 1943, as lawbreaking.
29. See Appendix 9.

the transfer of the Norwegian volunteers as their own *SS* Volunteer Mountain Brigade to near-home Finland (Karelia). Similarly Mussert,[30] the leader of the NSB in the Netherlands, had had reservations—though of a different kind—against Himmler's plans. He did not want the volunteers from Holland to fight in a "Nordland" Division, but in a "Nederland" Division.[31]

Because of these objections Himmler changed his plans. To replace the Norwegians being removed from the Division structure, Swiss volunteers of the *SS* Mountain Division "Nord" were to be transferred to the *SS* "Nordland" Armored Grenadier Division. The structure of the new *SS* units to be formed thus appeared as follows:

I. III (Germanic) *SS* Armored Corps, with
SS Armored Division "Wiking"
SS Volunteer Armored Grenadier Division "Nordland"[32]
(Danes, Germans, Swedes, Swiss)
II. *SS* Volunteer Mountain Brigade "Norge"

A short time later, Himmler changed his plans anew and opposed an exchange of the Swiss and Norwegian *SS* volunteers in the Karelian area. The approximately 150 Swiss remained in the *SS* Mountain Division "Nord," and the Norwegians in the III. (Germanic) *SS* Armored Corps.[33] As of June 28, 1943, the planned structure—still as that of an armored division—was to be as follows:

- Division Staff
- Armored Regiment with two units
- Armored Grenadier Regiment "Norge"[34] with three armored grenadier battalions

30. See Appendix 9.
31. Mussert's wish was met with the order to establish an *SS* Volunteer Armored Grenadier Division "Nederland." SS-FHA, Org. Tgb. No. 917/43 g. Kdos. of July 19, 1943.
32. The *Wehrmacht* command staff reported on July 25, 1943, that the 11. *SS* Volunteer Armored Grenadier Division would be ready for service as the central reserve of the OKW as of November 1, 1943.
33. In spite of that, the *SS* Ski Batalion "Norge" was formed in Norway in September 1943. The cadre consisted of the ski company formed in October 1942 of volunteers of the Norwegian Ski Organization at the urging of Norwegian Youth Leader Stang. The young Norwegians received their training first at the *SS* camp in Sennheim and later at the Police Weapons School I in Dresden-Hellerau. As of March 1944, the battalion served on the Kiestinki front and lost 165 dead and 135 missing by December 20, 1944. Compare Rolf Michaelis, *Die Gebirgs-Divisionen der Waffen-SS*, Berlin 1998.[2]
34. The cadre was the "Norwegen" Volunteer Division, plus parts of the *SS* "Nordland" Regiment; the number of Norwegian volunteers actually varied between 300 and 500 members. On September 15, 1943, there were 20 Norwegian officers, 50 NCOs, and 464 men in the 11th *SS* Volunteer Armored Grenadier Division "Nordland," and at the end of May 1944, 21 officers, 48 NCOs, and 269 men. At this time the *SS* Armored Grenadier Regiment 23 "Norge" had a strength of 1379 men.

- Armored Grenadier Regiment "Danmark"[35] (likewise)
- Armored Reconnaissance Battalion with two armored scout and two armored rifle companies,
- Assault Gun Battalion with three batteries,
- Artillery Regiment with three battalions,
- Flak Battalion with one 3.7-cm and three 8.8-cm flak batteries,[36]
- Tank Destroyer Battalion with three 7.5-cm companies (self-propelled mounts),
- Engineer Battalion with two (mot.) companies, one armored,
- Intelligence Battalion with one radio and one telephone company,
- Division Supply Chief with four fuel and four motor vehicle (120 t) companies,
- Motor Park Troop with three repair shop companies,
- Administrative Troop with one butcher and one baker company, provision and field post office,
- Medical Troop with two companies,
- Field Police Company.

Because of the difficulties of bringing the *SS* "Nordland" Armored Grenadier Division up to its planned strength—the Swedish volunteers[37] so grandly proclaimed by Himmler formed the IV. Platoon of the 3rd/*SS* Armored Reconnaissance Battalion 11—in June and July 1943 some 8000 ethnic German recruits from Siebenbürgen were ordered to the division.

The names of the two *SS* Volunteer Armored Grenadier Regiments "Norge" and "Danmark" were to offer the foreigners a "homeland." The question remained open as to in what sense the ethnic German soldiers, at more than 60% of the total strength, found a "homeland."

35. The cadre was the "Danmark" Free Corps. In mid-September 1943 there were 33 Danish *Führer*, 162 *Unterführer*, and 1191 men within the structure of the 11th *SS* Armored Grenadier Division "Nordland," and thus formed about half of the *SS* Armored Grenadier Regiment "Danmark." At the end of May 1944 there were 37 Danish officers, 220 NCOs, and 852 men. The total strength of the *SS* Armored Grenadier Regiment 24 "Danmark" at that time was 1503 men.

36. The *SS* Flak Battalion 11 was formed at the Arys-Nord troop training camp as of December 1, 1943, and transferred to Croatia outside the division structure. At the end of February 1944 the unit was to be moved to the Narva. In a serious transport accident, it suffered major personnel and materiel losses, and was ordered back to East Prussia for reformation. Only at the end of April 1944 did *SS* Flak Battalion 11 join the 11th *SS* Volunteer Armored Grenadier Division "Nordland" and see service at the Narva bridgehead.

37. This was a matter of centralizing the Swedish volunteers in the *Waffen-SS*.

Fritz von Scholz, Division Commander, *SS* Brigade Leader and Major General of the *Waffen-SS*.

Inspection of the training at Grafenwöhr.

The Chief of the 2nd/SS Armored Reconnaissance Battalion 11, *SS Obersturmbannführer* Heckmueller, at Grafenwöhr.

The Ethnic Germans from Romania

Only about 10% of the men in the 11th *SS* Volunteer Armored Grenadier Division "Nordland" were Scandinavian volunteers. Some 30% were native Germans, while the rest were ethnic Germans from Romania. Aside from some more or less large actions,[38] in which Romanian Germans were taken into German units in 1940-41, the mass of the ethnic German draftees served in the Romanian Army at first.

A change was suggested when, during the catastrophe of Stalingrad, thousands of ethnic German soldiers left their Romanian units and sought to join German forces. This led to a sharp note from the Romanian General Staff to the OKW on the subject of "desertion." The reason why they left the Romanian troops was primarily their ill treatment. Along with the obligatory physical punishment (beating), which generally applied to all minor charges, the ethnic Germans were still characterized as "German Hitlerists" and suffered numerous disadvantages. The German leadership, which was now very interested on account of the unreliability of the Romanian troops in taking the ethnic German "deserters" into the German forces, refused to return the men to the Romanian Army.

The *Wehrmacht* High Command, the Foreign Office, and the *Reichsführer-SS* (*SS* Main Office and Ethnic German Means Office[39]) even went a step farther and promoted the general release of ethnic Germans for German military service. Hitler took up the idea and, on May 12, 1943, agreed with the Romanian Marshal Antonescu on an "*Interstate Agreement on the Membership of Romanian Citizens of German Ethnicity in the German Army (*Waffen-SS*)*." Hitler's announcement that ethnic Germans from Romania would be resettled after the war had an influence that should not be underestimated.

The recruitment and enlistment took place via the Ethnic German Means Office and the Ethnic Group Agency in Romania. Although the majority of the eligible men volunteered, pressure was sometimes applied as well. The chief of the *SS* Headquarters, *SS Obergruppenführer* and General of the *Waffen-SS* Gottlob Berger, once expressed himself thus:

"*When an ethnic group has been led halfway passably, then they all volunteer freely, and those who do not volunteer freely simply have their houses wrecked. There are said to have been such cases in the Romanian Banat in recent days.*"

38. The first came to Germany in the so-called Thousand-Man Action in mid-1940 and formed the III. Battalion of the *SS Totenkopf* Division 16.

39. The Ethnic German Means Office was set up in 1936 as an administration of all available financial means for ethnic Germans, and was at first subordinate to the "Deputy of the Führer." On January 1, 1937, it was subordinated to the *SS* and *SS Obergruppenführer* Lorenz became its director. Additional tasks took place in 1939-40 with the settlement of ethnic Germans from Poland and the Baltics by the Ethnic German Means Office. The numerous resettlement camps served, among other things, in the recruitment of eligible ethnic Germans for the *Waffen-SS*.

Already as of May 20, 1943, transports rolled through Vienna to Germany. The *Waffen-SS* had reckoned on 20- to 30,000 men, but the result was twice as numerous, with around 60,000 ethnic Germans from Romania being gained for the *Wehrmacht* and *Waffen-SS* by the end of 1943. Hans Hedrich was one of the first volunteers:

"I was born in 1924 in Mediasch (Siebvenbuergen) and volunteered for the Waffen-SS *in 1943. I believed I must make my contribution to the German people's fight for existence—as the war was portrayed to us at that time. There was also a moral pressure from the organization of the 'German People's Group in Romania' and the social environment.*

Ordered to the SS *Armored Reconnaissance Battalion 'Nordland,' I was trained in Grafenwöhr. I found the training to be excessively hard. Despite all the chicanery in the training, it seems to have been strictly forbidden for the native German trainers to use denigrating expressions that hinted at the origins of the ethnic Germans.*

Generally there were no problems between the native Germans, us ethnic Germans, and the Scandinavians...."

The Transfer to Croatia

In view of the announced withdrawal of Italian units from the Balkans in the process of the shift of power in Italy, Hitler ordered on August 2, 1943, to transfer numerous forces from the homeland war zone to the developing vacuum. Into the realm of the "Southeast" Commander, the *SS* Armored Grenadier Division "Nordland," along with corps troops of the III. (Germanic) *SS* Armored Corps, were to be sent from the Grafenwöhr training camp, and the Jäger Training and Replacement Regiment from the Heuberg training camp, to the area south of Agram. After the SS-FHA reported on August 5, 1943, that the formation of the III. (Germanic) *SS* Armored Corps and the *SS* Armored Grenadier Division "Nordland" was not yet finished, the OKW first ordered the *Jäger* training and Replacement Regiment, and finally as of August 20, 1943, the III. (Germanic) *SS* Armored Corps with the *SS* Armored Grenadier Division "Nordland" to transfer to Agram. Although the *Wehrmacht* command staff still made clear on August 9, 1943, that the *SS* formations would not be ready for service until early in February 1944, the OKW, after conferring with the SS-FHA, subordinated the General Command of the III. (Germanic) *SS* Armored Corps tactically to the "Southeast" Commander just three days later. The units, though, should be called to active duty only according to the level of their formation and training, or occupy the Karlovac area in case it was evacuated by the Italians. The command post of the General Command of the III. (Germanic) *SS* Armored Corps was at first foreseen as Sisak or Petrinia.

On August 20, 1943, the first transports left the Grafenwöhr training camp, and at the end of the month they reached the Sisak area (some 50 km southeast of Agram). The units were divided in the area south of the Sava river:

- Division Staff, Sisak
- I. *SS* Armored Grenadier Regiment "Norge," Kostaynica
- II. *SS* Armored Grenadier Regiment "Norge," Bosanski Novi
- III. *SS* Armored Grenadier Regiment "Norge," Generalskistol
- I. *SS* Armored Grenadier Regiment 'Danmark," Glina
- II. *SS* Armored Grenadier Regiment "Danmark," south of Sisak
- III. *SS* Armored Grenadier Regiment "Danmark," Petrinia
- *SS* Armored Regiment "Nordland," Samobor and Yastrebarsko
- *SS* Artillery Regiment "Nordland," Dubica

Action in Croatia (September-December 1943)

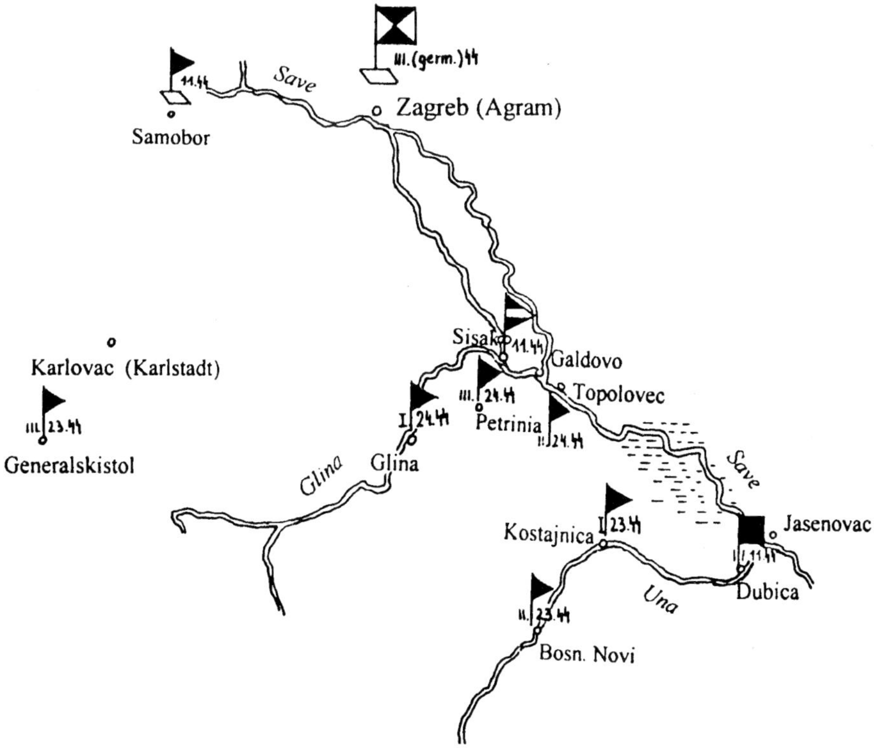

Along with further training, positions and road barriers against partisan attacks were built. Under the leadership of experienced soldiers, who were temporarily transferred from the 5th *SS* Armored Division "Wiking" to the 11th *SS* Armored Grenadier Division "Nordland," several units took part in the disarmament of Italian troops in the Samobor and Karlovac area.

In the summer of 1943, political tensions were added to the problems that existed throughout the restructuring. After the German-Danish relations in the spring of 1943 had steadily grown worse, caused in part by sabotage and the German reaction to it, and numerous strikes had put German control in Denmark to the question, an exceptional situation was proclaimed. One result was the disbanding of the Danish armed forces, which had still remained after April 9, 1940.[40] The Commanding General of the III. (Germanic) *SS* Armored Corps, *SS-Obergruppenführer* and General of the *Waffen-SS* Steiner,[41] wrote a euphemistic daily order on September 20, 1943, which is nevertheless a good reflection of the propaganda of the time:

"*1. With special joy and satisfaction, I have taken notice of the exemplary combat attitude in the Danish volunteers serving in the Danish regiment.*

2. I emphasize this particularly because the situation of the volunteers is not easy. You should know, though, that they can be fully contented with the situation of their members in the homeland, and that the increase in supply costs corresponding to the increasing expenses in Denmark will occur in the shortest time.

3. The political situation in Denmark is now completely quiet again. Life goes on normally. To be sure, the Danish Army is no longer on hand. The Armored Grenadier Regiment Danmark alone now embodies the Danish military tradition. I hope that the volunteers of the Armored Grenadier Regiment Danmark regard it as their greatest national treasure and are willing to have a Danish troop arise from this regiment, which, building on the combat experience of this war, represents not only a treasury of outlook and character but will also decisively influence the solution to the national and social problems in Denmark

4. For their present unshakeable, clear and characteristic unblemished, proud soldierly attitude I express my special recognition to the Danes, just as I would not expect anything different from Germanic men."

40. On October 6, 1943, the KTB/OKW recorded:
The condition of occupation created in Denmark on 29.8. is lifted again. The deportation of the former Danish armed forces is avoided. The evacuation of the Jews has produced statistics that are far behind the expected numbers of those left behind.
41. See Appendix 9.

Actually, though, many Danish volunteers were dissatisfied with their use. Many soldiers were eventually released in their homeland or transferred to Scandinavian units under Finnish command. Ingebret Lilleborge remembers:

"We had actually volunteered for service in Finland. Some were thus very dissatisfied with the transfer to Croatia. Several were even discharged from the SS *Armored Grenadier Regiment 'Norge' and transferred to Finland. New recruits from Norway arrived and calmed the perturbed German leadership.*

I had just returned from a training course in Kostaynica and was called to my Battalion Commander Vgt: 'You stay here to become a real soldier!'

The relationship with the population in Croatia was very good. Behind our positions, life went on very peacefully and normally—we protected them from the terror of the partisans. Our battalion was in the Kostaynica-Bos. Novi area on the Una River. The command post was in Kostaynica. The commanders lived in hotels or private quarters, while we built bunkers at our positions. The food was good, and we made do on the money. There were minor skirmishes with partisans but no real battles."

John Sandstad has similar memories:

"After the Volunteer Legion 'Norwegen' was disbanded, I was sent to SS *Armored Grenadier Training and Replacement Battalion 11 in Graz. There I took NCO training with nine other Norwegians. After a home furlough and several weeks as an instructor in an ethnic German recruit company at Graz, I was sent to* SS *Armored Grenadier Regiment 23 'Norge' in Croatia on November 2, 1943. Many of the Norwegian volunteers were disappointed because their was no exclusively Norwegian unit like the Legion or the Norwegian* SS *Ski Battalion in Finland.*

The ethnic Germans came in a group in August and made up some 50% of the unit's strength. Basically, we had good contact with them."

In October 1943 the regiments of the *Waffen-SS* were numbered. While the division had already been designated—at least sometimes—as the **11th** *SS* Volunteer Armored Grenadier Division "Nordland," the two armored grenadier regiments received the following numbers:

- *SS* Volunteer Armored Grenadier Regiment 23 "Norge" (Norwegian No. 1)
- *SS* Volunteer Armored Grenadier Regiment 24 "Danmark" (Danish No. 1)

At the end of October 1943 the *SS* Armored Reconnaissance Battalion 11 (*SS Hauptsturmführer* Saalbach) received its first armored personnel cars, which were used to motorize the 2nd and 5th Companies. Functioning as mobile alarm units, these two companies took part frequently in fighting partisans.[42] A former member recalls:

"On October 23, 1943, there was a big explosion about 3 km away, along with heavy MG fire. The alarmed 2nd Company, though, did not see action. On the next day there was an alarm in the midst of a maneuver ball that the 2nd Company was holding. The company got ready to fight and was transferred some 40 km down the Sava with all available vehicles. In an advance on a partisan camp there was very little contact with the enemy. The camp was deserted except for two men.

The 5th Company was attacked directly twice by partisans: a sentry was shot in the darkness, and another time a hand grenade was thrown into the sentries' sleeping quarters—fortunately without effect."

On November 1, 1943, the *SS* Armored **Regiment** 11 was restructured. The former II. Battalion, which had, among other things, disarmed an Italian armored regiment in Presco, near Agram, left the regiment and formed, as Heavy *SS* Armored Battalion 103, a corps troop of the III. (Germanic) *SS* Armored Corps.[43] Thus, only one *SS* Armored **Battalion** 11 remained in the division.

On November 20, 1943, Yugoslavian partisans attacked the 450 members of the I. *SS* Volunteer Armored Grenadier Regiment 24 "Danmark" near Glina. Because of enemy superiority, the Battalion Commandeer, *SS Sturmbannführer* Fischer, decided to take his companies back to Petrinya two days later, with no success. On November 24 and 25, 1943, there was heavy close combat in Glina. As parts of the II. and III. *SS* Armored Grenadier Regiment 24 "Danmark" advanced to support them, the III. Battalion had to be withdrawn at once all the same in order to march to another danger area—Hrastovica. Only after the use of dive bombers could the strongly pressured I. Battalion be freed, as the partisans withdrew into the mountains. The combat around Glina left 41 dead, 38 injured, and 2 missing. *SS-Obergruppenführer* and General of the *Waffen-SS* Steiner recognized the deed of a Danish *SS-Unterscharführer*, who had fallen in action, in a special corps order. Note that bands (i.e., partisans) were not spoken of, but rather Bolsheviks. Essentially it is a frightening example of what spirit was expected from the soldiers:

"The SS-Unterscharführer *N. O. Christensen, 1.* SS *Armored Grenadier Regiment 24 'Danmark,' after heavy fighting with superior enemies on 11/22/1943, fell into the*

---

42. Four- and eight-wheeled scout cars (Sd.Kfz. 222 and 231) followed in January and February 1944.

43. In January 1944 the Heavy *SS* Armored Battalion 103 was ordered to Kampen, near Zwolle, and received six Panzer VI (Tiger I) tanks for training purposes on February 4, 1944. After trained tank crews had been sent to other *SS* armored battalions again and again, retraining for the Tiger II tank and transfer to the Sennelager troop training camp followed at the end of August 1944. After receiving the first ten Tiger II tanks, the three companies were formed together into the Heavy *SS* Armored Battalion 503.

hands of the Bolshevik enemy. Before the Bolsheviks could search him, he reached into his trouser pockets, in which he had two hand grenades, and set them both off. The explosion shattered SS-Unterscharführer *Christensen, the four* SS *men standing around him, and all the Bolsheviks surrounding him.*

SS-Unterscharführer *Christensen has shown the sign of the highest heroic courage and deserves to live on in the ranks of his regiment as an example of the highest bravery, scorn of death, and high Germanic attitude. In the units of the Germanic Corps, his death will be a symbol of the highest action for the great Germanic Idea to all young soldiers, a sign of soldierly manliness to inspire emulation and live on in the history of the Germanic Corps.*"

Heinz Twesmann describes his military path to Croatia:

"*Born in 1920, I joined the LAH on April 1, 1937, and served as of May 1938 in the newly formed* SS *Standard 3 (later renamed 'The Führer' Regiment). On August 8, 1941, I was awarded the Iron Cross II during the battle at the Yelna bend, and was wounded in a shock-troop action on September 20, 1941. I received the wound decoration in black and was promoted to* SS-Oberscharführer. *On January 13, 1942, came my transfer to Holmestrand as an instructor to the volunteer Legion 'Norwegen.' After the transfer to Mitau, in Latvia, in the autumn 1942 there followed, in April 1943, the march to the Grafenwöhr troop training camp for the formation of the* SS *Armored Grenadier Division 'Nordland.' On May 1, 1943, I was promoted to* SS-Hauptscharführer.

In August of that year we were ordered to Croatia and spent several weeks in Kostaynica, on the Sava. Then we took quarters in Dvor, on the Una. There we were in the middle of a partisan area. All our supplies could be moved only in heavily armed convoys. Our unit formed the bridgehead for the III. Battalion, which was in Bosnisch Novi, on the Bosnian side of the Una. The Una was the old military border between Austria-Hungary and Turkey. Almost every night there was combat action with the partisans—we always had to be on the watch. During the day we conducted scouting activities in the partisan areas.

Once our battalion commander, the Norwegian SS-Sturmbannführer *Finson, came past during drill and said to me that the Norwegians did not need such a thing, that was a 'monkey theater.'*"

Swearing in at Hrastelnica on October 4, 1943.

Ethnic German recruits.

Tank training with a wooden model, Hrastelnica, November 18, 1943.

Training with VW amphibians on the Sava in the autumn of 1943.

Gun cleaning, Hrastelnica, October 29, 1943.

Getting food, Hrastelnica, October 20, 1943

From left to right, *SS-Untersturmführer* Erichsen, *SS-Hauptsturmführer* Saalbach, and *SS-Obersturmführer* Lorenz.

Securing the Croatian area.

Gun cars of the 5./SS Armored Reconnaissance Battalion 11 in Croatia, 1943.

Going to Sisak, 10/15/1943.

Fighting against partisans in the Sisak area, autumn 1943.

SS-Untersturmführer Langendorf in partisan action, September 1943.

Securing measures in Croatia.

Action in Russia

Because of the tense situation on the eastern front, Hitler already ordered on October 2, 1943, that the III. (Germanic) *SS* Armored Corps with the 11th *SS* Volunteer Armored Grenadier Division "Nordland" and the 4th *SS* Volunteer Armored Grenadier Brigade "Nederland"[44] replace an exhausted eastern division and troops from Army Group B. In the process of preparation for this, an additional change regarding the subordinated *SS* units took effect. Though Himmler intended at first that the General Command of the III. (Germanic) *SS* Armored Corps should also direct the 5th *SS* Armored Division "Wiking," he changed his mind later and, instead, integrated Baltic formations. The KTB/OKW thus maintained:

"*Considered at this time is the transfer of the III.* SS *Armored Corps out of the southeastern area to Army Group North, along with the Baltic* SS *units,*[45] *of which the* Reichsführer-SS *assumes that they will fight well, since it concerns their homeland.*"

Despite the intervention of the Southeast Commander, who did not want to release the *SS* units until the spring of 1944, Hitler made it clear on November 21, 1943, that the troops were to be transported to the 18th Army in the east as of November 24, 1943. The last transport left Croatia, which Cossack units took over, in January 1944. This disturbed the Croatian population very much, as they feared for their freedom and property.

The first parts of the division reached their terminal depot on the Narva-Volossovo early in December 1943. While the missing vehicles and other items for the 2nd and 4th companies of *SS* Armored Reconnaissance Battalion 11 were arriving, the General Command of the III. (Germanic) *SS* Armored Corps made a request to the superior Army Command 18 on December 14, 1943:

"*The* SS *Armored Battalion 11 'Hermann von Salza'*[46] *was left behind in the area west of Agram as a full personnel battalion, since equipping with Panther or Panzer IV tanks and transferring of them to an armored troop training camp in the transport of the General Command of the III. (Germ.)* SS *Armored Corps was not yet ready. At this time the* SS *Armored Battalion 11 'Hermann von Salza' is subordinate to the 371st Infantry Division, XV. Mountain Army Corps, Pz. A. O. K. 2, Belgrade.*"

---

44. As of October 25, 1943, the order to establish the *SS* Volunteer Armored Grenadier Division "Nederland" had gone out of power, and in place of it, the *SS* Volunteer Armored Grenadier Brigade "Nederland" was formed. SS-FHA, Org. Tgb. No. 1612/43, g. Kdos. Of October 26, 1943.

45. This applied particularly to the later 20th Weapon Grenadier Division of the *SS* (Estonian No. 1). See also Rolf Michaelis, *Esten in der Waffen-SS*, Berlin 2000.

46. Named after the Grand Master of the Teutonic Knights.

Meanwhile, the proposed equipping of the SS *Armored Battalion 11 'Hermann von Salza' with assault guns has been ordered, with some of the assault guns already underway to the Oranienbaum front. Since Assault gun Battalion 11 is presently in the formative stage and is not in a position to have the final total of 45 assault guns, there is a danger that if the* SS *Armored Battalion 11 'Hermann von Salza' is not transferred immediately, some of the assault guns must remain immobile.*

The SS *Armored Battalion 11 'Hermann von Salza' is, according to its state of training, in the situation to take over the assigned assault guns fully, and can, after a short familiarization period, be regarded as fully ready for action.*"

The General Command of the III. (Germanic) *SS* Armored Corps took over the command of the 9th and 10th *Luftwaffe* Field Division, the battle group of the *SS* Police Division, and the 11th *SS* Volunteer Armored Grenadier Division "Nordland," also arriving from Croatia, on the hitherto quiet front of the Oranienbaum Pocket.[47] The 4th SS Volunteer Armored Grenadier Brigade "Nederland" was listed as still "*being transported to the 18th Army*" on December 26, 1943. The Romanian German Karl Balint remembers his first days on the eastern front:

"*The actual establishment of our formation staff took place only at Sisak, Croatia.I myself was with it from the start, meaning already in the summer of 1943 at Grafenwöhr-Auerbach, where I came to the 5th Company and received my basic training.*

In my home town of Schaessburg, Romania, I had already finished a course in automobile locksmithing and brought some knowledge with me to Grafenwöhr. After the short basic training was finished it was asked who had a driver's license, and I reported along with several other men. Then we went to Spielfeld, in Styria, and received military drivers' licences of all classes.

After that we went directly to Sisak. In the former hat factory there, the actual formation of the I-echelon began. Some Führer *and* Unterführer *were already present, as were some men.*

At the end of November and beginning of December 1943, the SS *Armored Reconnaissance Battalion 11 was sent by rail to Russia. Some of the first actions were already made, and we had to follow with the tractor. The chaos on the roads was great. We had a problem with the gearboxes of the amphibians, and logically, also with the* Kübelwagen. *In many dismantlings of the gearboxes it was found that the shift hooks were bent. The long shift levers put too much pressure on the shift hooks, which bent them. The shift lever was then simply shortened some 10 cm and it worked again. This was also reported directly to the VW factory. One of our exploits was that we removed the VW motor within the record time of seven minutes...*"

47. This was a Russian bridgehead held since 1941 and supported by the fortress of Kronstadt. The so-called Ingermannland was flat and swampy.

About the right-hand neighbors of the 11th *SS* Volunteer Armored Grenadier Division "Nordland," the *Luftwaffe* field units 10th Field Division (L) (Major General von Wedel)[48] and 9th Field Division (l) (Colonel Michael),[49] another member of the division wrote:

"On December 18, 1943, the Company Chief, SS Obersturmbannführer *Heckmueller, and I as Company Troop Leader, drove to the nearest positions of units of the 10th Field Division (L), to get a look at the situation. What we experienced made us shake our heads. In view of the nearby front at the Oranienbaum Pocket, at which, according to a battalion chief, scarcely a shot had been fired in a year and a half, we found luxuriously furnished quarters. The chief was not in a position to show us the exact course of the front line on a map, since according to his own statement he was only 'forward' once, to give a front examination group a look at the Soviet lines.*

Our 1st and 2nd Companies were in the same village. We received the rest of our winter clothing—we really lacked nothing. Missing weapons also arrived. The infantry gun platoon of the 5th Company[50] received its guns. But live ammunition was not yet on hand—the intelligence devices for the platoons and companies were also lacking. Training could thus only be continued in theory.

On December 21, 1943, in an isolated school, the unit carried out a map game in the presence of the Division Commander, in order to get acquainted with the region."

At the end of December 1943, the Division Commander reported the following strengths to the Inspector-General of the Armored Troops:

Officers	NCOs	Men	Helpers	Total	
618	2877	10,704	880	15,073	full
341	1975	10,146	106	12,568	actual

Thus, the unit had about 80% of its full strength. In all, there were 22 Norwegian *Führer*, 48 *Unterführer*, and 705 men in the division. At the same time, the Dames numbered some 1100 volunteers. There were about 40 Swedes. The unit, which was originally to be made up of Danes, Norwegians, and Swedes, consisted of almost 90% ethnic Germans. In a comparison between full and actual strengths, the unit lacked about 2500 men. Since almost 1200 of them were officers and NCOs, men were constantly commanded from appropriate schools.

48. See Appendix 9
49. See Appendix 9.
50. The 5th Company was a heavy company with one each engineer, 7.5-cm Pak 40, infantry gun, and cannon platoon. The last had the Assault Gun Cannon 39.

The materiel equipment in no way corresponded to that of an armored grenadier division. 96 planned Panzer III and IV tanks were lacking.

	Full	Actual
Assault Guns	31	30
Panzer III	3	0
Panzer IV	93	0
Armored Personnel/Scout Cars	167	141

As for trucks, only 30% of the total tonnage was on hand. On January 9, 1944, the *SS* Armored Battalion 11 "Hermann von Salza" too over the Panzer V "Panther"[51] tanks of the 4th *SS* Volunteer Armored Grenadier Brigade "Nederland" located at the site. The judgment of *SS* Brigade Leader and Major General of the *Waffen-SS* von Scholz gave further insight into the situation of the 11th *SS* Volunteer Armored Grenadier Division "Nederland":

"The level of training of the division, on the whole made up of recruits in June-July 1943, is characterized by the fact that the division, after brief recruit training at the troop training camp, was transferred to the Croatian area for further training and securing against partisan bands. The nature of the action limited the unit's training only to platoon strength. The resulting securing tasks required training in defense. Since their transfer to the Oranienbaum pocket, the unit's training has been carried on by the battalion in reserve and waiting to be relieved, which always takes up three weeks, so that after a period of 18 weeks (end of April 1944) it can be regarded as finished. The mood of the troops is excellent.

Special difficulties are caused by the too limited shipments of fuel, which rule out training in motorized groups. Unfilled positions in personnel, especially notable in the artillery, must be filled to a high degree. The division is suitable for limited tasks and for limited defense..."[52]

On January 14, 1944, the Red Army began its winter offensive at 7:00 AM in the area of the III. (Germanic) *SS* Armored Corps. With crushing superiority, the 2nd Soviet Assault Army broke through the positions of the two field divisions (L) on the right edge of the pocket. Farther to the east, the Soviet 42nd Army was also able to break through the L. Army Corps between the 126th and 170th Infantry Divisions the next day.

While the mass of the 11th *SS* Volunteer Armored Grenadier Division "Nordland" remained in its positions,

- the *SS* Armored Reconnaissance Battalion 11,

51. KTB of the 4th *SS* Volunteer Armored Grenadier Brigade "Nederland."

52. This contradictory statement that the unit was ready for attacking but only limited defense can be explained by the intention of the division commander to show the superior positions that the unit should be supplied with more materials quickly.

- the I./ *SS* Armored Grenadier Regiment 23 "Norge,"
- the I./ *SS* Armored Grenadier Regiment 24 "Danmark,"
- the I./ *SS* Armored Grenadier Regiment 48,[53]
- the *SS* Engineer Battalion 11

were transferred,[54] in order to clean up the enemy breakthrough in the 10th and 9th Field Divisions (L). When *SS Obersturmführer* Lorenz (Chief, 1./*SS* Armored Reconnaissance Battalion 11) found out by means of a scouting troop how far the enemy had advanced, it was already in the Ropsha area (15 km north of Gubanizy). Since the 1st Company scarcely had any ammunition, the 2nd/*SS* Armored Reconnaissance Battalion 11 received their order to advance via Klassino and Altbor to Dyatlizy. There they met demoralized, retreating soldiers of the two former *Luftwaffe* field divisions. Only with great difficulty were the men of the *Waffen-SS* able to get them to stop. A member remembers:

"*In Dyatlizy we found the command post of a* Luftwaffe *battalion, which must have been deserted in a panic. Despite preparations to blow it up, they had not even destroyed the secret command materials. We secured the site to the north and northwest and prevented the further advance of the Ivans. The company had its first losses.*"

Another focal point of the Soviet attacks was near Malkunova (west of Ropsha, 17 kilometers south of Oranienbaum). Here the *SS* Engineer Battalion 11, which had been ordered there (*SS Sturmbannführer* Fritz Bunse), held up the advance of the enemy troops for three days—the 2nd company alone reported 100 dead and wounded on January 14, 1944. In the building of urgently needed defensive positions, an Army engineer battalion whose members were all over 45 years old was subordinated to the *SS* units.

The I./*SS* Armored Grenadier Regiment 23 "Norge," held in reserve at Lopuchinka, began a counterattack on January 15, 1944, along with parts of the *SS* Assault Gun Battalion 11 and *SS* Artillery Regiment 11. Heinz Twesmann (3./*SS* Armored Grenadier Regiment 23 "Norge") was wounded in the fighting:

"*The 3rd Company did not take part in the attack on Sayostrovia with the 1st and 2nd Companies. Von Bargen led us toward Gostilizy in the darkness when suddenly, from a grove about 100 meters left of us, MG fire was heard and some* Luftwaffe *soldiers came running out. Von Bargen ordered me at once to reconnoiter toward the woods. We moved forward cautiously until we saw six T34 tanks standing at the northern edge of the grove. But they did not notice us, and we went into position some 50 meters ahead of them. At daybreak the tank farthest to the left began to shoot at the Rendemann Company. Our company was scarcely fired on, but von Bargen was wounded and I took over the company. At first I told the Battalion to use antitank weapons, but they were shot up before they could get off a single shot.*

53. 4th *SS* Volunteer Armored Grenadier Brigade "Nederland."

54. For this, the II./*SS* Volunteer Armored Grenadier Regiment 49 was subordinated to the Division.

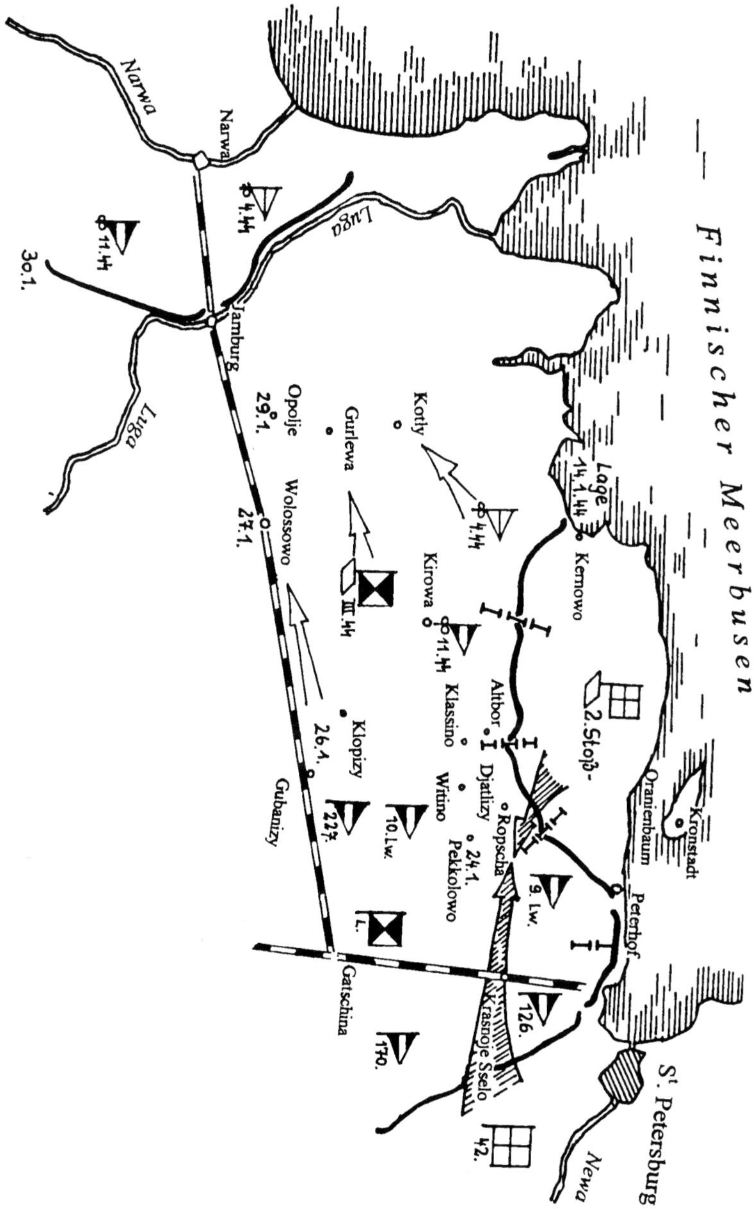
Finnischer Meerbusen
Narwa
Narwa
Luga
Luga
Jamburg
30.1.
Opolje
29.1.
Gurlewa
Kotly
Lage
14.1.44
Kernowo
Wolossowo
27.1.
Kirowa
Altbor
Klassino
2. Stoß-
Klopizy
26.1.
Djatlizy
Witino
Oranienbaum
Kronstadt
Ropscha
24.1.
Pekkolowo
Gubanizy
10. Lw.
9. Lw.
227.
Peterhof
Gatschina
Krasnoje Sselo
126.
170.
42.
St. Petersburg
Newa

Then came the command to detach ourselves from the enemy and gather south of the grove. There came an assault-gun battery, with which I was to attack via a gap in the woods. I took a place on the gun of SS Hauptsturmführer *Ellersick, who observed the terrain before us through a shear scope.*

Suddenly our gun was hit and we flew down. Running, we reached our old positions at the edge of the woods. SS-Hauptsturmführer *Ellersick could be rescued later, wounded. The T34s standing before us now began to fire on my 3rd Company, whereupon I gave the men the order to fire their carbines into the vision slits of the tanks. We could always withdraw.*

In a low spot, just south of the wood edge, we took up a position, and yet received direct grenade-launcher fire and a salvo from Stalin organs. Fortunately, we suffered no losses. I spotted an advanced Soviet observer in the trees and had all the company's machine guns take the treetops under fire. Shortly thereafter we saw a Red Army man fall to the ground. From then on it remained quiet, so that we could withdraw to the battalion's command post. This was in an earth bunker near an 8.8-cm Luftwaffe *flak battery. Scarcely had we gone into position when we received heavy large-caliber artillery fire. One gun near me took a direct hit, with dead and wounded. I was badly wounded by a splinter in my lung. That was on January 17, 1944.*"

John Sandstadt (1./*SS* Armored Grenadier Regiment 23 "Norge") remembers the combat in January 1944:

"*On the day of the major Soviet attack, our company had a strength of 118 men: 7 native German NCOs, 34 ethnic German men, 1 Flemish* Unterscharführer, *and 76 Norwegians (2 officers, 15 NCOs, 59 men). Our 1st Company also had the greatest number of Norwegians.*

On the night of January 15, 1944, the first enemy movement took place, and the counterattack in the morning completely collapsed under Soviet crossfire. We immediately lost 13 dead and many wounded. It was the same for the 2nd and 3rd Companies. All the same, we were finally able to hold our positions for some ten days, with our three companies being reduced to the strength of one company.

My brother Olav, born in 1921, had also registered for the Volunteer Legion 'Norwegen' on April 28, 1943, and served in the heavy platoon of our company; he fell in the Kosherizy area after five days. His last resting place was in the former division cemetery near Begunizy, between St. Petersburg and Narva.

When we had some rest on January 27, 1944, our company consisted of one Obersturmführer, *5 NCOs, and some 35 men. Our Battalion Commander Fritz Vogt appeared and handed several soldiers—including me—the E.K. II. Less as recognition for brave deeds than as a 'premium' for having survived the last 12 days.*"

Although the AOK 18 gave the German troops permission to withdraw on January 18, 1944, large parts of the 9th Field and 126th Infantry Divisions were surrounded. The Soviet 43rd Rifle Division (2nd Assault Army) and the 189th Rifle Division (42nd Army) had succeeded in forming a pocket around the German troops northeast of Ropsha. In heavy fighting in the Vitino area, 15 kilometers southwest to 30 km west of Ropsha, parts of the 11th *SS* Volunteer Armored Grenadier Division "Nordland" broke the pocket line and allowed most of the enclosed troops to join the withdrawal of the III. (Germanic) *SS* Armored Corps in the direction of Narva. Ingebret Lilleborge was wounded on January 23, 1944:

*"Our counterattack in the area of the 10th Field Division (L) on January 15, 1944, had shattered. Retreating somewhat, we dug ourselves in. But soon the Russians discovered our heavy machine-gun position and shot in on it. A grenade hit me there on January 23, 1944. After several days I was sent to the rear on my own. It is a crazy story how I, in the chaos on the road, sometimes on foot, sometimes in various vehicles, came to Narva and was taken by train from there to the hospital in Tallinn. While I was there, the hospital was bombed by the Ivans, and many patients died. Through its action on the Leningrad-Narva road, our Battalion (I./*SS *Armored Grenadier Regiment 23 'Norge') was practically shattered, and was formed anew in Germany. Released from the hospital, I reached Narva and the 9th Company (III. Battalion) early in March 1944."*

With attacks on the *SS* Armored Grenadier Regiment 23 "Norge" in the Saroshina and Mortinovz areas, the enemy showed his intention of cutting off the III. (Germanic) *SS* Armored Corps' retreat to Yamburg (Kingisepp). On January 28, 1944, Soviet armored units were able to catch up with the flanks and quickly enclose parts of the 11th *SS* Volunteer Armored Grenadier Division "Nordland" some 45 km east of Narva on the Kotly-Gurleva-Opolye line. While the *SS* Armored Grenadier Regiment 24 "Danmark" was subordinated to the 4th *SS* Volunteer Armored Grenadier Brigade "Nederland," the other parts of the division, along with what remained of the 10th Field Division (L), fought vigorously on both sides of Yamburg. Finally, the withdrawal over the Luga position in the direction of Narva could be continued. Franz Bereznyak (*SS* Armored Reconnaissance Battalion 11) tells of the fighting in January 1944:

"On January 30, 1944, we were before Narva. Kaiser and Pehrsson were wounded—the company was led by SS Oberscharführer *Hoegg. Who had ever thought that in the course of two weeks our proud unit would look like this?"*

Positions near Mummasaare, February 1943.

SdKfz 231 with 2 cm KWK 38.

"Bunker Street."

Mummasaare.

Fallen Russians in the field, February 1944.

A bunker on the Gulf of Finland, Mummasaare, February 1944.

"Well camouflaged."

SPW "Caesar" with 2 cm KWK and MG 42.

The Action of the *SS* Armored Reconnaissance Battalion 11 in the "Wengler" Battle Group

On January 22, 1944, the *SS* Armored Reconnaissance Battalion 11 was subordinated to the group of Colonel Wengler[56] (Commander of the 18th Army's Weapons School), which was hit hard and could scarcely defend itself. When Colonel Wengler ordered the *SS* Armored Reconnaissance Battalion 11 to attack an enemy assemblage near Pekkolovo, *SS Hauptsturmführer* Saalbach formed two battle groups:

- Battle Group "South" (*SS Obersturmführer* Heckmueller) with the 2nd and 3rd Companies, plus *Wehrmacht* units;
- Battle Group "North" (*SS Obersturmführer* Schmidt) with the 1st, 4th, and 5th Companies.

The two battle groups moved out from Pekkolovo and were able to push back the Red Army men, who were surprised by the German counterattack. A former member recalls:

"*In a dip we observed Russian infantry and horse-drawn vehicles that formed 2 or 3 columns. Our cannons, antitank guns, and machine guns began to fire immediately.*

Since the village now seemed to be free of enemies, we wanted to scout farther. Suddenly heavy German artillery fire began and wounded several men, especially in the 4th Company. Our battle group regarded the goal as attained and began to withdraw with three damaged SPW in tow. SS Obersturmführer *Viehmann took over the 4th Company,* SS Untersturmführer *Langendorf the 5th Company.*"

When further reconnaissance disclosed a massive assemblage of Russian tanks in the area farther south near Gubanizy, the entire *SS* Armored Reconnaissance Battalion 11 was thrown into that area. From west to east there were the 1st, 2nd, 3rd, and 4th Companies, with the Antitank Platoon on the outside. On the night of January 26, 1944, an enemy tank brigade with 54 tanks and an infantry battalion with 350 men attacked the place. The antitank guns and the cannon platoon were able to shoot down 34 tanks, including 28 T-34. The Hollander, *SS Rottenführer* Caspar Sporck, shot down 11 tanks himself and received the Knight's Cross for it. Friedrich Höpfinger was wounded in the battle:

"*The weather was foggy and dull, with snow cover. With my messenger Maier I went forward to scout the terrain and decide on the position for my infantry gun platoon. A fireball before me ended my efforts. But a splinter hit the right side of my neck, went through my esophagus, and stuck in my neckbones, just on the right side. My white camouflage*

56. See Appendix 9.

*suit turned very red. When Maier crept up, I asked him, expecting to lose consciousness, to notify my wife. My voice was very different, since a vocal cord was also injured. But nothing happened, and Maier brought a nearby SPW. I asked the driver to drive with me to my platoon's position, so I could turn over command to then-*SS Sturmmann *Krämer. It was not easy to take leave of my men. They all stood there with drooping shoulders, and I had to leave them. That scene always remained in my memory.*"

The other companies of the *SS* Armored Reconnaissance Battalion 11 were fighting then against the accompanying infantry battalion. In a decoration proposal for the German Cross in gold for *SS Obersturmführer* Lorenz one can read:

"SS Obersturmführer *Lorenz had the task in the Wengler Battle group at Gubanicy on January 26, 1944, of securing the western part of Gubanicy. Despite the heaviest enemy tank attacks, Lorenz was able through his personal example to call on his men again and again to the last opposition and hold the commanded line.*

During this combat he had placed himself behind his MG, and thus set an example to eliminate any thought of giving up the threatened position. He had contributed significantly to keeping his own supply route, which was available for the Wengler Battle Group, open long enough to maintain the tactical situation."

After the withdrawal of the entire 18th Army was ordered on the same day, the 4th Volunteer Armored Grenadier Brigade "Nederland," on the western edge of the pocket, at first drew back to Kotly. While the mass of the 11th *SS* Volunteer Armored Grenadier Division "Nordland" withdrew via Kirova, in the direction of Gurleva and Opolye, the transferred units, after fighting between Klopizy and Gubanizy, moved back to the Volossovo area. The town of Volossovo, fired on by Stalin organs, was especially important for its railroad depot. Colonel Wengler equipped *SS Obersturmführer* Lorenz with an assault gun, two cannon wagons, one antitank gun, and two eight-wheel and two four-wheel scout cars, plus two armored personnel carriers of the 3rd and 4th Companies to hold the town as long as possible. Lorenz remembers:

"*Suddenly, Tiger tanks appeared. I still thought, 'Oh God, again, what is rolling over us,' since a tank had torn the whole box off the side of my four-wheel scout car, since the road was too narrow. They came, God knows from where, out of the Russian lines and towed some of their own vehicles. But these Tigers had prevented the Russian tanks from making a complete mess of us at Volossovo.*"

After Volossovo was given up by German troops on the evening of January 27, 1944 the withdrawal to the west went on—a front that hung together no longer existed. On January 29, 1944, there was heavy fighting again near Opolye, in the course of which two more enemy tanks would be destroyed. On the next day the men were already before the Estonian border along the Narva. The then-*SS Sturmmann* Toni Ging remembers the difficult withdrawal days:

"*After the arrival of* SS *Armored Reconnaissance Battalion 11 before Oranienbaum in mid-December 1943, the 3rd Company was housed in a small town. We finally received our armored troop transporters here. The majority were open vehicles, but a few had a turret and a 2 cm cannon and MG 34. Since I was trained as a driver, I was given such an SPW. The commander was an* SS Rottenführer, *and the gunner was a Swedish comrade. I have unfortunately forgotten both their names.*

We also experienced the tank battle near Gubanizy on January 26, 1944, and were ordered to make the dismounted crews of the disabled enemy tanks harmless. Our SPW was near a 7.5 cm cannon car and a Pak of the 5th Company, and I saw through the hatch that SS Obersturmbannführer *Langendorf was giving his orders to the men. In the evening we were used as a rear guard, along with other SPWs of the 3rd Company. Our vehicle was one of the last to leave Gubanizy.*

On January 27, 1944, we were near Volossovo, and were assigned to reconnoiter a village. We were accompanied by an SPW with armored grenadiers. The road led us to a narrow road in the direction of the village. Some 1200 meters before the town I drove my SPW to the right side, to be able to give covering fire to the grenadiers. They reached the edge of town at the same time—until then, not a shot had been fired.

Since no enemies were to be seen, the other SPW went back, and I also turned to go back. Scarcely were the grenadiers at our level when we came into heavy infantry fire from the village. I drove onto a heap of stones, which had been hidden under the snow, and thus got stuck. The fire became heavier and heavier, and we absolutely had to leave the vehicle. First the commander up in the turret, then the Swede, and then I, the driver. Ducking down, we ran to the other SPW, which waited for us. But before we arrived, the Swede was hit. We crept to him and pulled him to the SPW. It drove as fast as it could to a wood edge some 300 meters away and stopped there. There I saw my own SPW blow up. We went on to the main dressing station—unfortunately, our Swedish comrade died of his injury. Our 3rd company still had a fighting strength of 25 men at that time!"

When they reached the Estonian border, the subordination of the *SS* Armored Reconnaissance Battalion 11 to the command of the Wengler Battle Group ended. Thus, they returned to the 11th *SS* Volunteer Armored Grenadier Division "Nordland."

The Commander of the *SS* Armored Reconnaissance Battalion 11, *SS Sturmbannführer*

A light armored radio car, SdKfz 261, with frame antenna.

An eight-wheel armored scout car, Sd.Kfz. 231.

SdKfz 250/9.

Fighting in Estonia

On February 4, 1944, the newly-formed Army Battalion "Narva" took command of the III. (Germanic) *SS* Armored Corps and the XXVI. Army Corps (Lieutenant General Grasser). The new HKL ran at that time from the coast near Hungerburg along the Narva around the German bridgehead at the city in a southwesterly direction. A former division member remembers the first action on the Narva:

"*Action of the 2nd Company to stabilize the front in Narva and to the north. 4 to 6 SPW at a time (one a command car) drive up behind the front line to give the infantry the feeling of a stabilizing backbone. We are supported by a Tiger of the Army. Losses include a direct hit on a scout car and one on the forward MG of my command car (MG bent 90 degrees, cast iron shield splintered).*"

When Soviet troops tried to take the town of Merekuela in a surprise attack by landing from the sea on the night of February 13-14, 1944, the Artillery Leader of the III. (Germanic) *SS* Armored Corps, *SS* Brigade Leader and Major General of the *Waffen-SS* Kryssing, in command of the "Coast" Battle Group,[57] called for support from the 11th *SS* Volunteer Armored Grenadier Division "Nordland." They sent Armored Reconnaissance Battalion 11 into the threatened area. A former member remembers:

"*At 4:00 AM alarm, take everything with you and get aboard. We went toward the road, on which we met other units. In Merekuela the Russians had landed from the sea, and in fact at the spot where the Navy had taken up a gun position. The coast at the landing place was some 30 meters high, very steep. At 7:00, when the danger had already been eliminated by us, 12* Stukas *appeared from Wesenberg. By 2:00 PM everything was over.*"

In mid-February 1944 the 11th *SS* Volunteer Armored Grenadier Division "Nordland" received replacements for the first time, and could thus fill their decimated units. The Division's strength report at the end of February 1944 gave the following picture:

Officers	NCOs	Men	Helpers	Total
564	3028	11,545	880	16,017 full
102	1785	9247	9	11,143 actual

The hard fighting from mid-January 1944 on was shown by the losses: by the end of February 1944, nine officers and 403 other ranks had died, and 1240 division members had been wounded. In the actual figures, there were also 1679 wounded, sick, or missing

57. The "Coast" (Küste) Battle Group consisted of, among others, an Estonian police battalion, two coast artillery batteries, and the two naval battalions "Hohnschild" and "Schneider." The strength at the time was actually about 9000 men.

included, so that the actual strength was 9464 men. Thus, the Division did not even have 60% of its full strength. The shortage of officers and NCOs was particularly noticeable: they lacked 462 officers and almost 1300 NCOs. *SS* Brigade Leader and Lieutenant General of the *Waffen-SS* von Scholz sent a critical report on this to the SS-FHA:

"*The fighting value of the Division was decisively influenced by high losses of officers and NCOs, which is all the more serious because of the few officers and NCOs available when it was established. In the composition of the Division (Germanic volunteers from Denmark, Norway, Sweden, and the southeastern area), the fighting value rises or falls depending on the elimination of this shortage.*

The meager motorized mobility (25% of the full vehicle numbers), along with the fully available weapons and equipment on hand at its formation (including winter equipment), has in the withdrawal movement led, despite the setting of the keenest demands, to the border of physical capability on the men, to extraordinarily high weapon and equipment losses. In the further mobile action of the Division, further losses are to be expected because of the decrease of the available vehicles.

The training level of the replacements arriving in the report month did not allow their inclusion in the fighting troops. Further training with the Field Training Battalion (4 to 6 weeks) was necessary. The physical and spiritual condition of the replacements is good.

The flak battalion is still being trained at the troop training camp in Arys. Because of the loss of almost all optical devices and lack of towing vehicles, its readiness for action cannot be expected before May 1, 1944.

The enclosed war structure gives a twisted view, since according to AHM 43 of 12/21/1943, 27th edition, the number of 890 total wounded, sick, or missing—1679 men of the fighting strength—must still appear in the 'actual' list. Thus, about 10% of the complement is missing from the Division.

The mood of the troops is good, even though the political development in Denmark and Norway has not remained without a reverse effect on the Germanic volunteers from those countries.

Until sufficient filling out with capable officers and NCOs, the Division has only limited capability for defense."

The materiel equipping was catastrophic, including *SS* Armored Reconnaissance Battalion 11:

	Full	Actual
Assault Guns	73[58]	10

58. The 73 assault guns were to be apportioned as follows: *SS* Assault Gun battalion with three batteries of 11 assault guns and *SS* Armored Battalion 11 "Hermann von Salza" four companies with 10 assault guns each.

Panzer III	3	0
Panzer V	0	3
Armored Personnel & Scout Cars	25[59]	117

At the beginning of 1944 the full equipping of the Division by the SS-FHA was changed. While the Division was originally—as a planned **Armored** Division—to have 31 assault guns, three Panzer III, and 93 Panzer IV tanks, plus 167 armored personnel carriers and scout cars, the full figures were cut in February 1944 to a total of 76 armored combat vehicles (assault guns and Panzer III) and 25 armored personnel and scout cars. The actual numbers, though, looked very different. The Division had only 10 assault guns (*SS* Armored Battalion 11 and *SS* Assault Gun Battalion 11), but had three Panzer V "Panther"[60] tanks and 92 armored personnel and scout cars.

Heinz Gensow was among the first replacements in February 1944:

"We came from the SS *Field Training Battalion 11 as replacements to the* SS *Armored Reconnaissance Battalion 11, which was at Mummasaare, on the Gulf of Finland. We young faces were introduced to the commander,* SS Hauptsturmführer *Saalbach; the Adjutant,* SS Untersturmführer *Erichsen, and the Ordnance Officer,* SS Untersturmführer *Schmitz were also present. A division among the companies was carried out. I remained, with a few others, in the staff as messengers. We were still at rest on the Baltic Sea coast. None of us newcomers had been at the front before, so we had no such experience.*

SS Hauptsturmführer *Saalbach was often on the way to situation discussions with the Division or other units. Thus I, as a messenger, also came to a company in the foremost position at Narva and had my first contact with artillery and infantry fire. Then the quiet time by the sea was over.*

The SS *Armored Reconnaissance Battalion 11 went back into action. The withdrawal from Narva began. The companies of the Battalion were often drawn far apart by their actions—here today, many kilometers away tomorrow. Now we messengers were in action constantly. I soon knew every map of the action sites by heart."*

On March 12, 1944, *SS Hauptsturmführer* Saalbach and *SS Untersturmführer* Langendorf were awarded the Knight's Cross to the Iron Cross for the withdrawal fighting from the Oranienbaum Pocket. The Commander of the 227th Infantry Division, Lieutenant General Berlin,[61] wrote in the award application for *SS Hauptsturmführer* Saalbach:

59. The full number of 25 armored personnel and scout cars was not to be reached. Just the *SS* Armored Reconnaissance Battalion 11 was to have some 15 vehicles per company. With five companies and a staff company, this meant about 90 vehicles! There were also motorized companies of the two Armored Grenadier Regiments.
60. They had been taken over in January 1944 from the area of the 4th *SS* volunteer Armored Grenadier Brigade "Nederland."
61. See Appendix 9.

SS *Gruppenführer* and Lieutentant General of the *Waffen-SS* Kleinheisterkamp awards Knight's Crosses at Hungerberg.

SS *Untersturmführer* Georg Langendorf.

From left to right: *SS Sturmbannführer* Saalbach, *SS Untersturmführer* Langendorf, *SS Hauptsturmführer* Seebach, and *SS Hauptsturmführer* Krügel. Hungerburg, March 19, 1944.

Bunkers in the woods at Soolkuela, April 1944.

Assault guns roll up near Soolkuela, April 1944.

Firing position near Soolkuela, April 1944.

"Forest" landscape near Soolkuela, April 1944.

Visible at the rear, the symbol of the 11th SS Volunteer Armored Grenadier Division "Nordland."

A soldier reads the Narva front newspaper in 1944.

A gun car of the 5./SS Armored Reconnaissance Battalion 11, still with chalk coating.

"*The action of the* SS *Armored Reconnaissance Battalion 11 was of decisive importance for the acticity of the 227th I.D.* ["Wengler" Battle Group, mid- to end of January 1944; author's note]. *Very special recognition was earned by the personal action of* SS Hauptsturmführer *Saalbach, who through his bravery and imperturbability gave a glowing example. Saalbach is very particularly worthy of being awarded the Knight's Cross to the Iron Cross.*"

The Red Army, which had already formed a bridgehead at Kriivasao, south of Narva, at the beginning of February 1944, was able to break through the positions of the 170th and 227th Infantry Divisions on the Lauke Swamp and push forward in the direction of Veivara and Auvere. Since the Soviet troops were not able to break through the 61st Infantry Division, fighting between the 170th and 227th Infantry Divisions, the so-called "west sack" (170th Infantry Division) and "east sack" (227th Infantry Division) were formed.

The Army Battalion "Narva" ordered the immediate shattering of the two front bulges and ordered parts of the 11th *SS* Volunteer Armored Grenadier Division "Nordland" into the threatened area. The *SS* Volunteer Armored Grenadier Regiment 24 "Danmark" remained in the Narva bridgehead and was subordinated to the 4th *SS* Volunteer Armored Grenadier Brigade "Nederland," which was known as the "Wagner" Group in the ensuing time. The parts of the 11th *SS* Volunteer Armored Grenadier Division "Nordland" called the "Scholz" Group (especially *SS* Armored Grenadier Regiment 23 "Norge" and *SS* Armored Reconnaissance Battalion 11) at first marched into the area of the 61st Infantry Division.

On March 17, 1944, the troops of the Soviet 8th Army in the "west and east sacks" went on the offensive again to break the Tallinn-Narva road. In the so-called "west sack" the Red Army reached Rivimaa via Dirgala. In heavy fighting lasting some six days, parts of the *SS* Armored Grenadier Regiment 23 "Norge" (*SS Obersturmbannführer* Fritz Knöchlein)[62] and *SS* Armored Reconnaissance Battalion 11 were able to push the enemy back again on swampy ground. In the "east sack" the German units, with help from the heavy Armored Battalion 502 (Panzer VI "Tiger"), prevented a further break into their positions.

On March 26, 1944, the 11th Infantry Division, along with the heavy Armored Battalion 502 and parts of the "Strachwitz" Armored Unit (Colonel Count Strachwitz)[63] composed of *SS* Armored Reconnaissance Battalion 11, advanced into swampy terrain to smash the "west sack." When the Soviet units made a counterattack the next day, three days of back-and-forth fighting ensued. On March 30, 1944, the enemy finally evacuated the region. The OKW reported it without going into the very high German losses:

62. See Appendix 9.
63. See Appendix 9.

"Southwest of Narva, in several days of hard offensive fighting in roadless wooded and swampy land, with effective support from artillery, smoke screens, tanks, and fighter planes, the mass of several Russian divisions was surrounded and destroyed. Repeated enemy attempts to escape were crushed. In these battles the enemy lost over 6000 dead, several hundred prisoners, 59 guns, and numerous other weapons and equipment of all kinds."

The so-called "east sack" was also to be pushed back, beginning on April 19, 1944, by the "Strachwitz" Armored Unit, plus the 61st Infantry Division and battle groups of the 122nd and 170th Infantry Divisions, as well as the "Feldherrnhalle" Division. After five unsuccessful days with heavy losses, the "Narva" Army Unit ordered the halting of the attack. The front now ran just north of the Piata to the Narva south of Auvere, and bent in a southerly direction after some 16 km, ran through the Lauka Swamp to Omati, and then back to the east shore of the Narva.

In the same time period, the two First Battalions of the *SS* Armored Grenadier Regiments 23 and 24, shattered in the previous battles, were withdrawn from action and sent to be reestablished at the Hammerstein troop training camp. But the two battalions were not to return to the 11th *SS* Volunteer Armored Grenadier Division "Nordland," but remained under the command of the 5th *SS* Armored Division "Wiking"[64] from November 1944 on. The 11th *SS* Armored Grenadier Division "Nordland" thus had only four armored grenadier battalions.

The *SS* Assault Company 103 also fought in the ranks of *SS* Armored Grenadier Regiment 24 "Danmark" (*SS Sturmbannführer* Wilhelm Krügel) at the Narva bridgehead at that time. The Belgian *SS* volunteer Andre Hellebuyck, who was court-martialed, also fought in the Probation Unit of the III. (Germanic) *SS* Armored Corps. At the end of April 1944, Hellebuyck ended up on the front after spending time in Danzig-Matzkau, Dachau, and the Probation Battalion of the *Waffen-SS* in Chlum near Selchan, and has been missing since those battles. In a last letter he wrote to his mother:

"At 1:00 AM we—a whole company—arrived at the battlefield and replaced other boys. We sit here at the beginning of Russia and the end of Estonia. But what the place is called, I cannot say. I don't know. Mama, we are here in the foremost trench, but you don't need to worry, for I am making sure that they [the enemy; author's note] *cannot see me. The Russians sit here some 400-500 meters away from us, but at night they come up to 100 meters. But Mama, before they get that close, I have already seen them all and shot them*

64. See the chapter "The First Battalions of the *SS* Armored Grenadier Regiments 23 and 24," in the group of the IV. *SS* Armored Corps.

After the area of the Army Battalion "Narva" had become more quiet at the end of April 1944, the Commander of the 11th *SS* Volunteer Armored Grenadier Division "Nordland" took command of the "Wagner" Group. This still led the *SS* Armored Grenadier Regiment 24 "Danmark" on the right wing near Dolgaya-Niiva in the Narva bridgehead. Until the summer of 1944 there were mutual scouting troop undertakings and a relatively quiet immobile war.

With the war coming to an end in Finland (Armistice on September 5, 1944), the Red Army took forces from there to the Narva front. Since the German command reckoned on an attack from the Kriivasao bridgehead to the north to cut off Narva, the front was taken back up to a barrage line ("Tannenberg Position") between the Peipus Lake and the Gulf of Finland.

The Battle on the Narva Front and in the Tannenberg Position (February to September 1944).

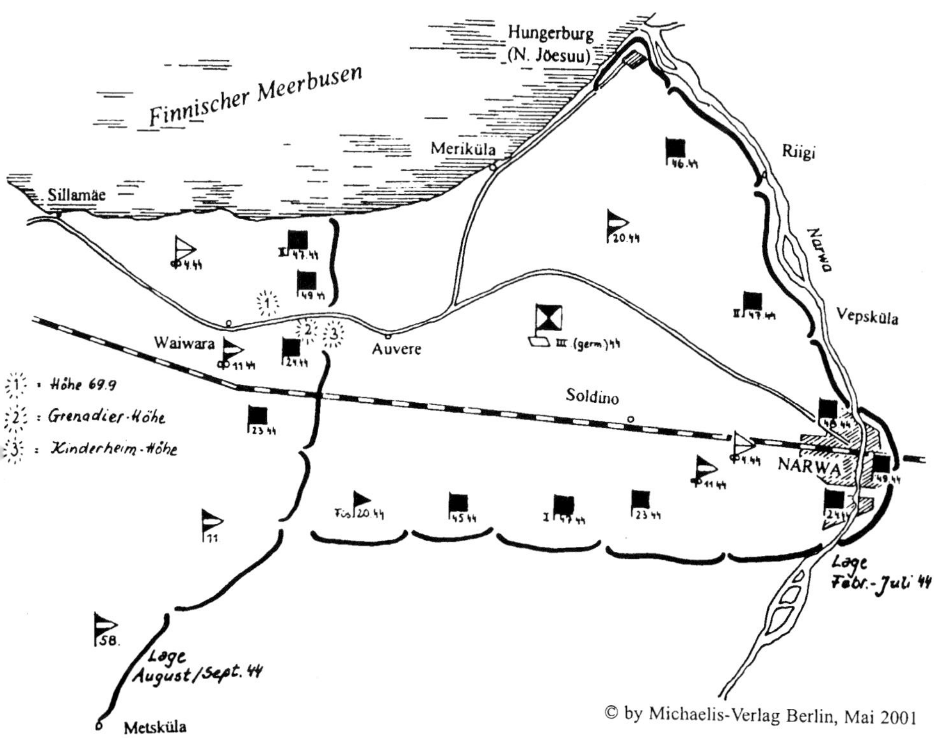

The 11th *SS* Armored Grenadier Division "Nordland" consisted on June 30, 1944, of:

Officers	NCOs	Men	Total
612	2877	10,704	14,193 full
355	1857	8,788	11,000 actual

Although the unit, with about 3000 men (1300 of them officers and NCOs), had gaps and only about 75% of full strength, it proved to be above average in strength compared to other German divisions. The listing above lacks the two 1st Battalions of the *SS* Armored Grenadier Regiments 23 and 24, which were being reformed at the Hammerstein troop training camp.

On July 12, 1944, the first commands were given to occupy the "Tannenberg Position." Two days later the Chief of Staff, III. (Germanic) *SS* Armored Corps, *SS Oberführer* Ziegler,[65] cancelled the orders. The *SS* Armored Grenadier Regiment 24 "Danmark" had to fight off especially heavy attacks at the Narva bridgehead in those days. Soviet breakthroughs at battalion strength would, though, be turned back by midnight on the evening of July 15, 1944, with support from two assault guns and three artillery batteries. But 20 soldiers were lost, 50 wounded, and one went missing.

In the night of July 24-25, 1944, the withdrawal to the "Tannenberg Position" finally began. At 11:30 PM the "Wagner" Group vacated the Narva bridgehead. Immediate Soviet advances from the Hungerburg and Kriivasao area to the Narva-Tallinn retreat route were held off by the *SS* Armored Battalion 11 "Hermann von Salza." In order to cover the transfer of the slower, partly horsedrawn artillery, the *SS* volunteer Armored Grenadier Regiment 49 was assigned a battery of the *SS* Assault Gun Battalion 11, among others. The other batteries were used individually as support in the area of the 11th *SS* Volunteer Armored Grenadier Division "Nordland." While the *SS* Armored Grenadier Regiment 48 "General Seyffardt" withdrew from Narva as the rear guard and was shattered by the Red Army on the way to the "Tannenberg Position," the other troop units reached the new main battle line. Here the Blauberge, with the so-called Kinderheim and Grenadier Heights, and Hill 69.9 formed special defense points.[66]

The two battalions of the *SS* Armored Grenadier Regiment 24 "Danmark," along with the "Langemarck" Battle Group (Kinderheim Heights) and the II./*SS* Armored Grenadier Regiment 23 "Norge" (Grenadier Heights), occupied the area between the road and the railroad line. Southwest of there, below the Tallinn-Narva railroad, was the III./*SS* Armored Grenadier Regiment 23 "Norge." When the strategically important Kinderheim Heights were taken by Soviet units at 11 PM on 26 July, *SS Gruppenführer* and Lieutenant General

65. See Appendix 9.

66. The Estonian name of the Blauberge is "Sinimaed," those of the heights "Grenaderimaegi" and "Lastekodumägi."

of the *Waffen-SS* von Scholz arranged an immediate counterattack by 122 assault guns. The next day the Commander of the 11th *SS* Volunteer Armored Grenadier Division "Nordland" was hit in the head by a shell fragment and died on the way to a surgical special unit in Rakvere. The ex-Chief of Staff, III. (Germanic) *SS* Armored Corps, *SS Oberführer* Ziegler, took command of the Division.[67] On July 28, 1944, the Flemish and Estonian (I./Weapon Grenadier Regiment of the *SS* 47) members of the *Waffen-SS* fighting in the Kinderheim Heights area were again overrun by the Red Army. A counterattack of the II./*SS* Armored Grenadier Regiment 23 "Norge" could not prevent the focal points of the fighting on the Grenadier Heights to the west from being dispersed. On July 29, 1944, the enemy tried to finalize the victory with over 100 tanks. As *SS Obersturmbannführer* Kausch with his *SS* Armored Battalion 11 "Hermann von Salza" made a counterattack, there was vigorous tank fighting. In all, 113 Soviet tanks were shot down. The OKW reported the enemy losses on August 1, 1944. They were silent about their own heavy losses of men and materiel:

"*On the peninsula of Narva the enemy did not continue his major attack because of his heavy losses. Weaker attacks were crushed. Taking an outstanding part in the successful repulse of the Soviet attacks in the last days was the III. (Germanic)* SS *Armored Corps under the command of* SS Obergruppenführer *and General of the* Waffen-SS *Steiner, with the* SS *Germanic Volunteer Divisions 'Nordland' and 'Nederland,' the 20th Estonian* SS *Volunteer Division, the 11th East Prussian Infantry Division, and units of the Navy, Army artillery, and launchers on the land front.*"

On August 5, 1944, the Red Army tried again unsuccessfully to break through the German positions. A counterattack by the III./*SS* Armored Grenadier Regiment 24 "Danmark" and the *SS* Probation Company 103 brought even the Grenadier Heights back into German hands. Since the focal point of the Soviet attacks moved to the south, the "Tannenberg Position" became somewhat more quiet.

When Hitler decided to withdraw the German troops from Estonia, the III. (Germanic) *SS* Armored Corps, being regarded by Army Group North as its strongest unit, received the order to transfer at once via Pernasu to Latvia. The *SS* troops, in the course of the so-called Operation "Aster," at first occupied the Ranna-Puneria Purtse line, then moved southwestward to join the II. Army Corps via Vanakuela and Wesenberg. While the 11th *SS* Volunteer Armored Grenadier Division "Nordland," along with the 11th Infantry Division, moved quickly to Riga, the 4th *SS* Volunteer Armored Grenadier Brigade "Nederland" took over as the rear guard and detached itself from the enemy only on September 19, 1944.

67. *SS Obersturmbannführer* Bockelberg became the new Chief of Staff, III. (Germanic) *SS* Armored Corps.

Officers, NCOs, and men at Mummasaare in 1944.

Bunker of the Staff "Strippenzieher," taken at Mummasaare on July 7, 1944.

Iron Crosses II. Class are being awarded.

Quiet time during the action.

A "camouflaged" light armored personnel carrier, SdK 250/9.

The "Hermannfeste" in Narva.

The Danish *Untersturmführer* Mogens Schwarz.

Soldiers' graves on the Kinderheim Heights.

Memorial stones for those who fell on the Kinderheim Heights.

The Kinderheim Heights.

A 7.5 cm antitank gun.

Memorial stone and cross on the Blauberge (Tannenberg Position).

Sd.Kfz. 251 with a frame mounted to deflect fog shells.

The *SS* Armored Reconnaissance Battalion 11 at Jakobstadt and Dorpat

After the Soviet summer offensive had begun on June 22, 1944, the Red Army was able to advance toward Tukkum and Riga on 10 July in the area north of Vilna and south of Duenaburg, on the line between Army Groups North and Center. 29 rifle divisions and one armored brigade marched through the resulting 25-kilometer-wide gap between the 16th Army (Army Group North) and the 3rd Armored Army (Army Group Center) in the direction of the Baltic coast.

The Commander of Army Group North turned to Hitler, in order to withdraw the 16th and 18th Armies in the direction of Kovno and Riga to avoid their encirclement. The Army Unit "Narva," according to his plan, should be transported by sea to Memel. Hitler rejected this proposal and ordered that the connection between Army Groups North and Center be reestablished by all means. In addition, rolling up of Army Group North was to be prevented and the enemy forces were to be smashed—Utopian goals!

To do this, the General Command "Kleffel,"[68] at first called the "Kleffel" Seam Group, was formed of the Staff of Security Division 285 on the extreme right flank of the 16th Army. Their task was filling the empty space between the II. Army Corps (Army Group North) and IX. Army Corps (Army Group Center). The first troops (above all, the Barrage Unit "Riewald,"[69] and other parts of the 225th Infantry Division) were joined by the *SS* Armored Reconnaissance Battalion 11, which was loaded at the Waivara and Kohtla-Joehvi depots on July 11-12, 1944. On 13 July the units, after traveling through Wesenberg, Dorpat, Volmar, Wenden (Cesis), and Riga, arrived at Stockmannshof and Jakobstadt on the Duena, marching the next day across the border into Lithuania into the Rokiskis area. Via Kamayai the *SS* Armored Reconnaissance Battalion 11 reached Panevezys on July 22, 1944.

When the 61st and 58th Infantry Divisions were moved into the area at the same time, the General Command of the XXXXIII. Army Corps took over the area of the "Kleffel" Corps Group. The Corps' left border now ran by the Ssarty Lake, the right one in the Skapiskis area. On the extreme right flank—in hopes of finding a link with troops of the IX. Army Corps—the *SS* Armored Reconnaissance Battalion 11 was placed. Constantly moving in the area of the "Kleffel" Corps Group and the XXXXIII. Army Corps, it pretended to be stronger German motorized troops and frequently attacked the flanks of Soviet troops

68. See Appendix 9.
69. Kurt Riewald, as a Major and Commander of Grenadier Regiment 333 (225th Infantry Division), received the German Cross in gold on August 17, 1944.

The Action of the *SS* Battle Group "Saalbach" in Lithuania, July 13-August 1, 1944

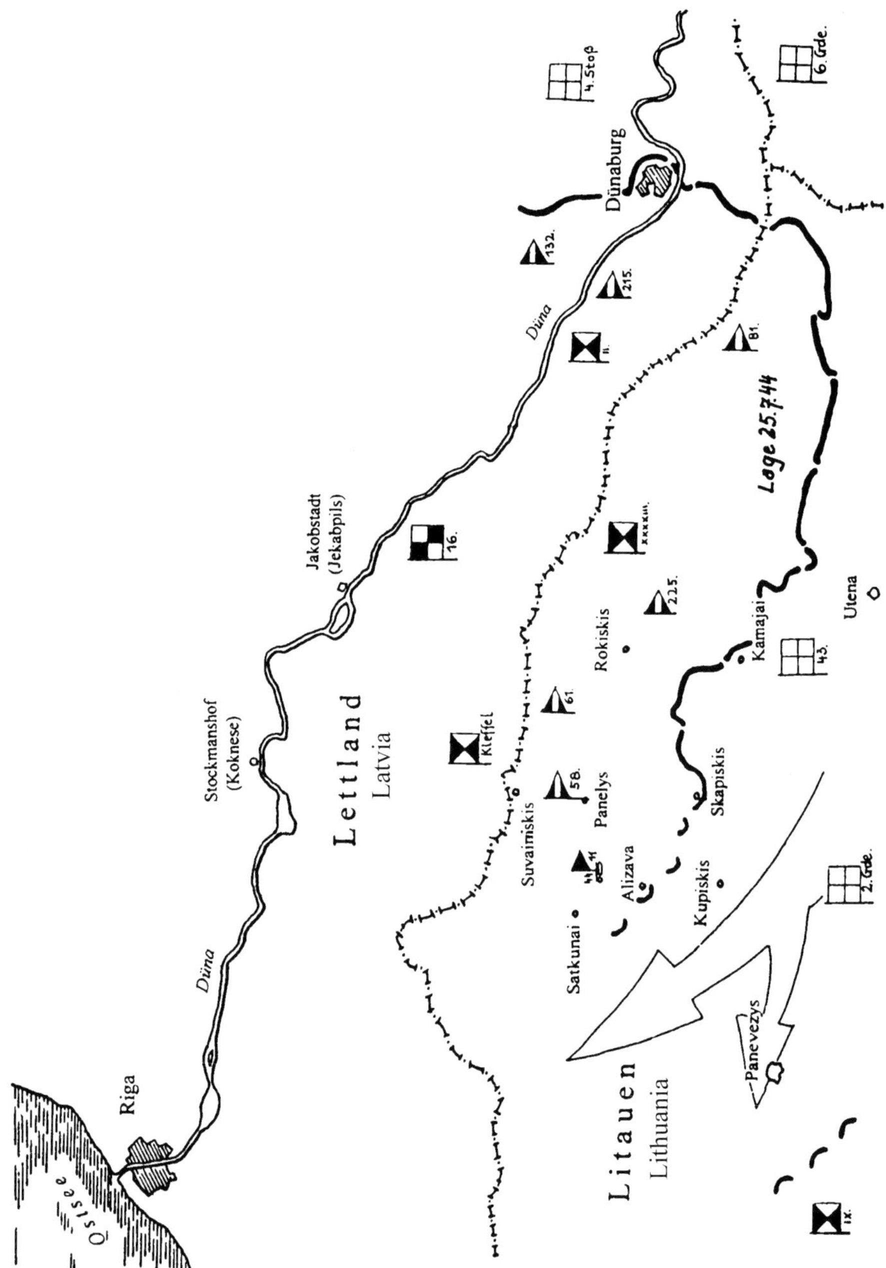

advancing toward Riga. The war diary of the General Command, XXXXIII. Army Corps, noted on July 22, 1944:

"Corps command post Abeli, enemy increases before the right flank, quiet in the 61st Infantry Division, several attacks with tank support on the left flank; focal point of attacks against the Army's left flank try to disturb the buildup of a new German front by surrounding and frontal attacks, retaking of the Army's left flank behind the Duena, final position: Drasviaty Lake, Duena shore south of Duenaburg, west bank of the Duena, Lievhof, south end of Luban Lake. Code name for this operation: Eulenspiegel.

Artillery Battalion 436, subordinate to heavy Armored Battalion 502 of the 58th Infantry Division, heavy Mortar Battalion 833 to 58th Infantry Division, SS *Armored Reconnaissance Battalion 11 has taken Ponemunial, I./Grenadier Regiment 151 (61st Infantry Division) to 58th Infantry Division, light Flak Battalion 735, II./ Flak Regiment 23 to 58th Infantry Division, Assault Gun Brigade 202 to 58th Infantry Division, gap closed in 225th Infantry Division, 61st Infantry Division hopes to reach commanded line. Armored Train 26 subordinated to 61st Infantry Division, Flak Barrage Unit is moved into the open right flank. Pandelay is taken, likewise Ponemuk."*

Three days later the *SS* Armored Reconnaissance Battalion 11 fought along with the I./Grenadier Regiment 154 (58th Infantry Division) in the Laukminskiai area. On July 28, 1944, when the new Commander of Army Group North, Senior General Schierner, gave the order to unload at the Marienburg position,[71] the *SS* members were already fighting near Satkunai. On July 31, 1944, the I. Army Corps relieved the "Kleffel" General Command. At the same time, the *SS* Armored Reconnaissance Battalion 11 was ordered back across Latvia to Estonia after its last combat near Siliski and Skrepiskis. Hans Stemper remembers the action in Lithuania:

"On the way—some 800 km in all—we enjoyed the beautiful region in fine weather. When we passed through Jakobstadt, now on wheels, the city was apparently empty of people. Our vehicles gathered at an intersection of the main street. While waiting, we learned that the stores had been plundered. Open doors, goods lying all around, even on the sidewalk.

Our task south of the Duena was to hold up the Soviet advance guard at Mitau-Tukkum, smash them if possible, and cover the south flank of Army Group North. Our course now led southward. Near Akniste we crossed the border into Lithuania. Only south of Urli, some 130 km southwest of Duenaburg, did the Battalion swing to the west, beyond Panevezys to the northeast. There were always fights and the danger of being exposed on the flank.

71. This linked the Duena with Peipus Lake.

On the evening of July 26, 1944, we stopped at a lake near Satkunai. The only building was a school. Judging by the setup, library, physics room, etc., it must have been a higher school with boarders. There was also a well-filled supply room. Under the roof hung hams, sides of pork, and sausages—scarcely believable. Everything was neat and clean, as if the students had just left the school. We did not consider plundering the supply room. It was probably because most of us regularly received parcels from home, meaning from the Banat or Siebenbürgen. For example, I always had food. Naturally, we also examined the nearby area, where we discovered some 300 men of the Todt Organization in a ditch. They sat or lay around apathetically, and had already come to terms with the prospect of imprisonment. Naturally, they were very happy when we turned up.

Battle alarm was heard south of the lake. The chief tank was carefully placed under cover behind the school. We were warned and remained in alarm readiness.... What we learned was that the enemy had broken through to the south. For us there remained only the way northward over a height. After this was also occupied by the enemy, we were surrounded. As if on the drill field, the entire Battalion turned out near Satkunai on July 27, 1944, to carry out the breakthrough. The heavy company went first, the rest of us followed...

Suddenly SS Obersturmführer *Langendorf called 'Pak in position, out at once!' The Chief and the Company Troop Leader sprang to the left, Borger and I to the right into the road ditches. Shooting while bent over, we moved forward. Only* SS Obersturmführer *Langendorf stood upright as always and observed the grain field. Slowly I came to believe that he was unwoundable.*

Since I had to reload I knelt down, and looked to the right to find out whether the Battalion had meanwhile spread out. Then I felt something hit me in the face, suddenly saw colorful circles that rushed toward me, ever faster and bigger. A sharpshooter had hit me. I thought 'now they've got me—what will Mother say?—no, you must not die now!' I turned around and showed Biorger my first-aid kit. Because of the wound I could no longer speak. Back at the SPW I was pulled inside by the driver and given emergency bandaging. In reverse gear we went back to the medical SPW. The medic, a countryman of mine, both born in Siebenbürgen, only 15 km apart, talked to me, calming me. He replaced the bandage and gave me an injection after I had made signs to him. I was carried away when I was awakened by shouts 'Breakthrough succeeded, we did it!'"

Erwin Schmaltz was also present at this action:

"When the central sector of the eastern front went to pieces in mid-June 1944, our reconnaissance unit was transported hastily by rail and thrown into the area vacated by German troops between Duenaburg and Jakobstadt. By constant movement we pretended to be a front that did not really exist. I still remember what Saalbach said when we came back from a Wehrmacht *commander's discussion. He told me he had the feeling that they wanted to stir us up—perhaps in view of July 20, 1944?*

As we drove through a town during this defensive fighting, an inhabitant informed us that there was a storehouse of German textiles, electric appliances, etc. Here the farmers had been able to trade their farm produce. Since it was only a matter of hours before the Russians arrived, I had him show me this building and had no thought of breaking into it. Using an SPW, we opened the door and were quite surprised at what we found there: women's sweaters, swimsuits, and silk hosiery, plus Bosch motorcycle dynamos. Those were all things that had not been available in Germany for a long time. I loaded myself with about 30 pairs of silk stockings, but only brought three pairs home to my wife—the word had gone around the staff of what treasures I had, and many—including the commander—asked me for a pair. Then we took a 50-kg bag of sugar and all the eggs that the farmers had already traded in. In the following days we had eggs and eggs again; soon they were hanging out our mouths."

Heinz Gentsow remembers:

"Near Jekapils (Jakobstadt) we were in a farmyard with part of the staff, and the companies were in positions some 2 km from the command post. Shelter holes and MG positions were built up, for the Russians constantly fired artillery into the area. Infantry-gun shells also whistled past us. At noon one day the artillery fire became heavier. Our position took several hits, and the barn burned down. Then came a company's radio message: Enemy attacks. The connection broke off, and SS Sturmbannführer *Saalbach wanted to send me to the company. This could no longer be done, as the first SPW of that company appeared to the right of our command post. There was noise everywhere, and we were attacked by Russian infantry. We could still hold them back with our machine guns, but then were also fired on from behind. The devil was loose. Then our Commander ordered 'Everybody back!' Our SPW drivers were ready, and everyone tried to get into a vehicle. I rode with the Commander in a VW, and while he drove, I pulled in my head and fired my machine pistol backward. Our VW was hit several times, but we managed to reach the other companies, which were just unloading. Then we had to pull back to the nearest town, from which we brought the Russians to a stop with a counterattack."*

At the beginning of August the *SS* Armored Reconnaissance Battalion 11 was transported by rail via Bauts, Meiden, Mitau, Riga, Wenden, Walk, Dorpat, and Johvi to Vaivara. There they were unloaded and marched to a quiet place in the area north of Metaguse.

When the front between Ostrow and the south end of Pleskau Lake had broken up on July 18, 1944, and the 3rd Baltic Front (General of the Army Masslenikov) attacked the XXVIII. Army Corps on the left flank of the 18th Army on August 10, 1944, the Red Army was able to reach the area east of Voru. They found no more German troops there at that time! The Army Battalion "Narva," ordered to bar the area between the Peipus and Wirz Lakes, ordered the newly subordinated 207th Security Division on August 14, 1944, to hold the narrows by Mehikoorma and southward as long as possible and set up a catching position to the south, in the Voehandu River area. A planned attack of the XXVIII. Army Corps to close the gap to the "Narva" Army Battalion was called off, since the troops to the north had already drawn back to the Voehandu position. In order to rebuild the link between the 207th Security Division and the troops of the XXVIII. Army Corps, orders were given on August 14, 1944, to form the *SS* Battle Group "Wagner." This unit of division strength, led by the Commander of the 4th *SS* Volunteer Armored Grenadier Brigade "Nederland," consisted of:

- *SS* Intelligence Company 54
- *SS* Field Police Troop 54
- *SS* Repair Shop Platoon 54
- I./ Weapon Grenadier Regiment of *SS* 45
- I/. Weapon Grenadier Regiment of *SS* 46
- II./ Weapon Grenadier Regiment of *SS* 46
- Battle Group 5th *SS* Volunteer Assault Brigade "Wallonien"
- Grenadier Regiment 23 (Army) of the 11th Infantry Division
- A battery of Army Coast Artillery Battalion 1004
- III./ Launcher Regiment 3
- II./ Artillery Regiment 58
- *SS* Armored Reconnaissance Battalion 11
- A company of *SS* Tank Destroyer Battalion 54

and marched into the area between the right wing of the subordinated 207th Security Division and the left wing of the XXVIII. Army Corps near Poelva.

The *SS* Armored Reconnaissance Battalion 11 was alarmed in view of the action in Metaguse, and moved via Mustvee and Maarja-Magdaleena in the direction of Dorpat. There the unit was supplied with fuel and ammunition. Then it marched on over the Embach bridge toward Raepina. On August 16, 1944, it had its first combat with Soviet troops, which had crossed Pleskau Lake, between Raepina and Mehikoorma. Fighting near Ignaste followed on 19-20 August. When the 3rd Baltic Front and the 54th, 67th, and 1st Assault Armies moved northward to break through between Dorpat and Valk on 21 August, the connection between the 18th Army and the "Narva" Army Battalion was broken. The *SS* Armored Reconnaissance Battalion 11 was in heavy fighting near Noo on that day.

The Combat in Southern Estonia between Wirz and Peipus Lakes

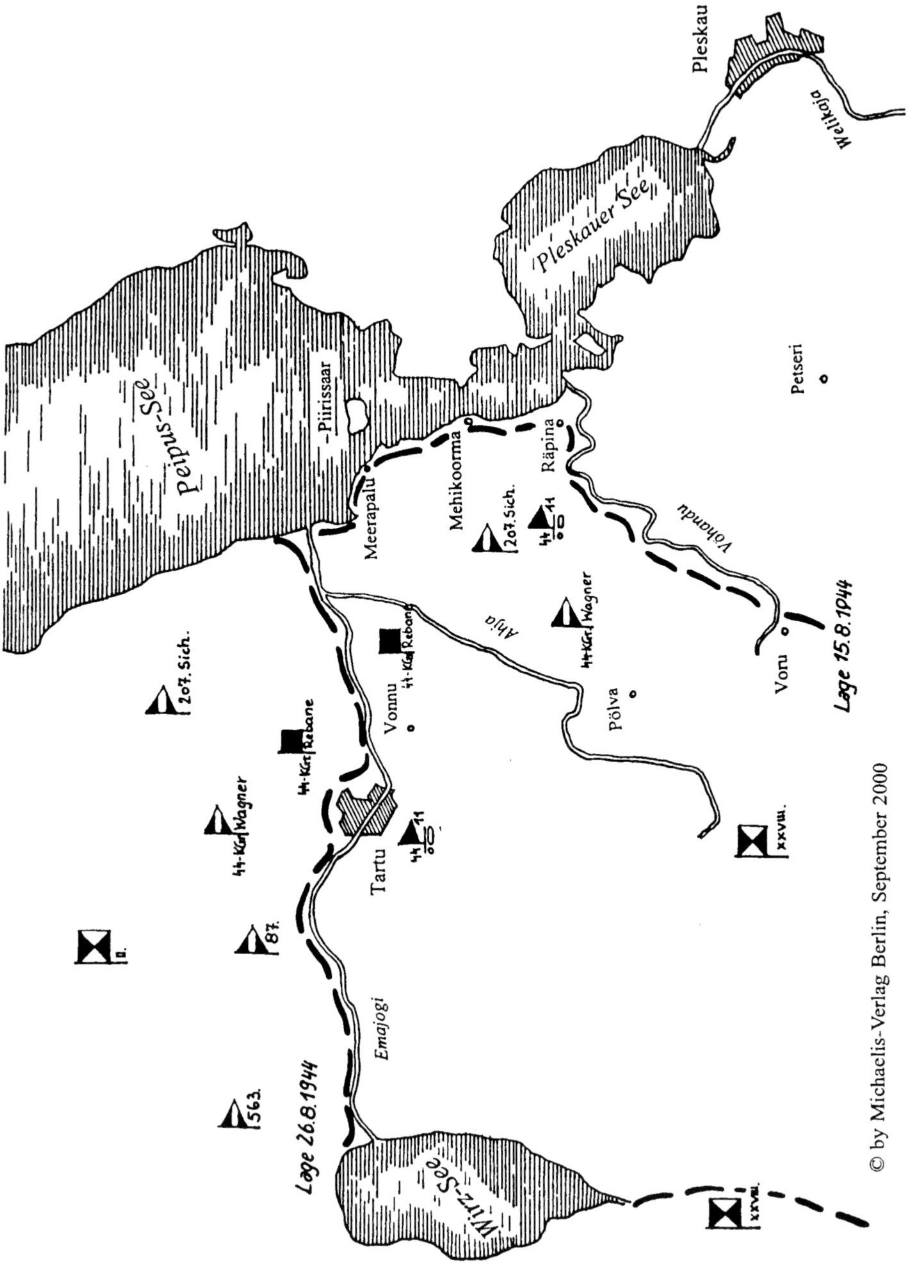

The German troops were now ordered to take up new defensive positions across the Embach. During isolated actions south of the river, with the *SS* Armored Reconnaissance Battalion 11, for example, in the Paeni area, the Red Army was able on August 24, 1944, to cross the undamaged Embach bridge near Karevere to the north. After brief, heavy fighting, the Soviet troops were able to occupy Dorpat, and had thus formed an important bridgehead.

Since the front sector along the Embach calmed down with the attainment of this goal—until September 17, 1944—the *SS* Armored Reconnaissance Battalion 11 was ordered to Metaguse via Kaerkna and Mustvee early in September 1944. Here the men again had several days of rest and were strengthened by Navy men. The then *SS Unterscharführer* Franz Bereznyk reports on the fighting in the Dorpat (Tartu) area:

"*We went into position near Ignaste on August 18, 1944. Strong Russian units, supported by tanks and self-propelled guns, were to take these heights to cut off the German troops in the Dorpat area. Our command post was in a doctor's house near Ignaste. Our men had dug in the armored personnel carriers on a hill, so that only the machine guns could be seen. From the hill we could observe the valley before us, in which the Soviets were getting ready in a small patch of woods. Shortly after 1:00 PM they came—15 tanks and several self-propelled guns, accompanied by strong infantry. To be sure, they did not suspect what they were approaching. Tensely we waited for the command to fire. Our Company Chief,* SS Obersturmführer *Pehrsson, observed it all through a shear scope. When the enemies reached the upward slope came the thundering command 'Fire!' And all 15 MG 42, a 2 cm flak gun, and a 7.6 cm cannon of the 5th Company, as well as numerous machine pistols and several grenade launchers from farther back began to fire. For the Russians it was an inferno—only a few were able, under the cover of the tanks, to get back to the protecting forest. In the evening the enemy tried again with cries of Hurrah—but in vain; we held our position. On August 23, 1944, we were then replaced by a* Wehrmacht *unit. Our new goal was Dorpat. Here the entire Reconnaissance Battalion was to make a major attack. At 3:00 it started. We rolled over the dug-in Russians hell-for-leather, until we suddenly were fired on from the left flank. A vigorous battle raged, with some losses—suddenly it turned out that they were Estonian comrades....*"

The Swedish *SS Untersturmführer* Hans-Goesta Pehrsson.

Action of the Saalbach Battle Group in Lithuania and Estonia.

The *SS* Battalion z.b.V. "Nordland" within the 4th *SS* Volunteer Armored Grenadier Brigade "Nederland"

In mid-September 1944 the *SS* Field Training Battalion 11 (*SS Obersturmbannführer* Lang) was renamed the *SS* Battalion z.b.V. "Nordland" and subordinated to the 4th *SS* Volunteer Armored Grenadier Brigade "Nederland" for the "Tannenbaum"[72] to replace the shattered *SS* Armored Grenadier Regiment 48. The first action was the occupation of the Pärnu (Pernau) bridgehead, along with the I./*SS* Armored Grenadier Regiment 49.

On September 23-24, 1944, the Battalion fought in the ranks of the hard-hit 21st Infantry Division and was located at Tilcens, partly without connection to a right or left neighbor. After no link with superior command posts could be made, the 4th *SS* Volunteer Armored Grenadier Brigade "Nederland" ordered an attempt to join the beginning withdrawal of the 21st Infantry Division. The *SS* Battalion z.b.V. "Nordland" was then placed in the Daibe-Pipeni line. Enemy attacks could be halted by counterattacks of the I./*SS* Armored Grenadier Regiment 48 and the *SS* Battalion z.b.V. "Nordland" near Purgaili. Since the assembly of the 21st Infantry Division was still in full swing, the attained line had to be held under all conditions. Numerous heavy attacks with tank support on the entire front of the *SS* Battalion z.b.V. "Nordland" compelled a withdrawal. Most of the motor vehicles had to be blown up for lack of fuel.

Still fighting against very superior forces, the *SS* Battalion z.b.V. "Nordland" was able to destroy two enemy tanks with antitank guns, two with close-combat means, and one by direct fire from a light infantry gun on September 25, 1944. Along with the I./*SS* Armored Grenadier Regiment 49, the "Barbara Position" was taken on the night of October 3, 1944. The Batallion of the 4th *SS* Armored Grenadier Brigade "Nederland" replaced the "Grossdeutschland" Grenadier Regiment on the night of October 5, 1944, along with the *SS* Battalion z.b.V. "Nordland," sometimes called the "Lang" Battalion.

On October 12, 1944, came the order for the 4th *SS* Volunteer Armored Grenadier Brigade "Nederland," within the III. (Germanic) *SS* Armored Corps, to be sent to the Libau area for offensive use. After a difficult night march on bad roads and paths, the Brigade was ready to attack in the area north of the Tirs-Purvs swamp two days later.

72. The "Tannenbaum" movement was the task of the "Tannenberg Position" and movement to Latvia.

The Brigade advanced in four shock wedges—the "Lang" Battalion moved forward only with great difficulty because of mines in the road, numerous Pak and grenade-launcher attacks, marksmen in trees, and large enemy forces. Attempts to go around the enemy failed, and the Battalion was taken back to its starting position. Only on October 16, 1944, was it able, after another attack, to drive the Soviet units out of the area south of Babriski. The 4th *SS* Volunteer Armored Grenadier Brigade "Nederland" was removed from the area of the 1st Army Corps after its action, and on October 17, 1944, it was again subordinated to the III. (Germanic) *SS* Armored Corps.

A week later, the *SS* Battalion z.b.V. "Nordland," designated *SS* Field Replacement Battalion 11, returned to the 11th *SS* Volunteer Armored Grenadier Division "Nordland." On October 28, 1944, it replaced what remained of *SS* Armored Grenadier Regiment 24 "Danmark" in Purmsati and remained with this regiment, sometimes in the main battle line, until the evacuation at the end of January 1945. The battalion's command post was located at Gulby.

Action of the *SS* Battalion z.b.V. "Nordland" with the 21st Infantry Division (September 23-26, 1944)

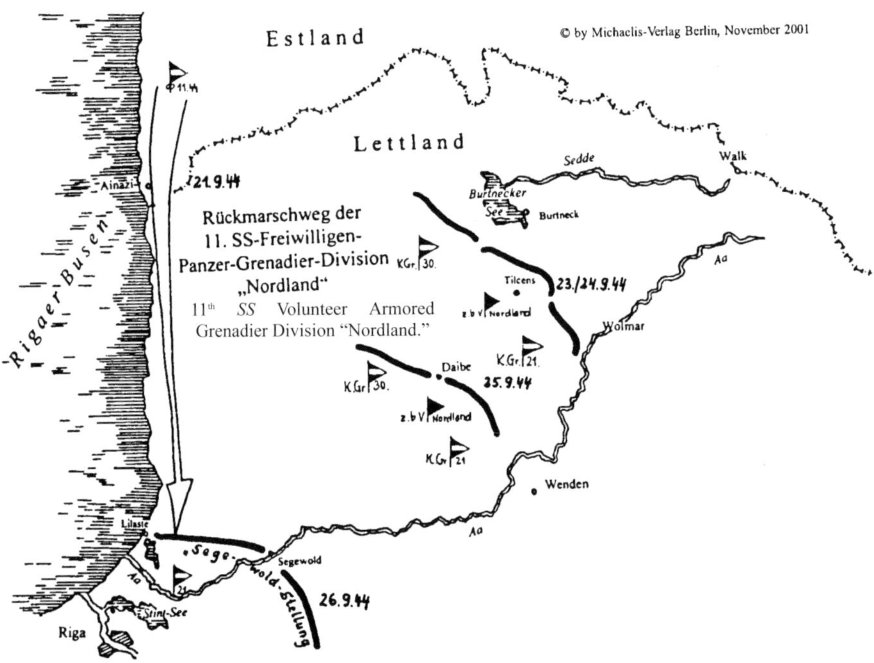

Action in Latvia

The fast transfer toward the Latvian capital, Riga, not only led the soldiers to the brink of exhaustion, but neither were the vehicles up to the burdens. The *Raupenschlepper Ost* tractors broke down, since they were too slow and not designed for long road marches in motorized units. Because the vehicles were overloaded with men, ammunition, weapons, and equipment, the tires blew, and patches were not available.

While the 11th *SS* Volunteer Armored Grenadier Division "Nordland" marched under these conditions, with only a strength of:

Officers	NCOs	Men	Helpers	Total
558	3391	12,612	931	16,561 full
328	1818	8,334	284	10,889 actual

Into the area—fought over vigorously since September 19, 1944—south of Riga, the remainders of the crushed divisions of the XXVIII. and L. Army Corps secured the withdrawal of the German troops from Estonia on the Valk-Volmar line. Although the 11th *SS* Volunteer Armored Grenadier Division "Nordland" had only 65% of its full strength, it was among the strongest units of Army Group North.

The *SS* Assault Gun Battery 54 was brought in with four assault guns of *SS* Armored Battalion 11—for them the 4th *SS* Volunteer Armored Grenadier Brigade "Nederland" received a Panther company of *SS* Armored Battalion 11 "Hermann von Salza."

The 11th *SS* Volunteer Armored Grenadier Division "Nordland" crossed the Estonian-Latvian border at Ainazi on September 24, 1944, and was ordered to the Baldone area to turn back the Red Army's assault on Riga, thus preventing the German troops to the northeast from being cut off. On the evening of the next day the units moved into the area south of the Kekava bridgehead formed by units of the 1st Army Corps. The General Command, III. (Germanic) *SS* Armored Corps led only the 11th *SS* Armored Grenadier Division "Nordland" and the 11th Infantry Division at that time. The task of the III. (Germanic) *SS* Armored Corps was to strengthen the weak front between the "Kleffel" Corps Group and the XXXIX. Armored Corps and gain time for further measures by a limited counterattack.[73]

After the Soviet attacks ran their course, the German units began their own offensive on September 23, 1944. The *SS* Armored Grenadier Regiment 24 "Danmark" was subordinated to its right neighbor (14th Armored Division), and the *SS* Armored Grenadier Regiment 23 "Norge" formed the left flank to the 11th Infantry Division. Until September 26, 1944, there

73. These three corps were gathered into the "Grasser" Army Battalion on September 25, 1944.

was very heavy back-and-forth fighting with enormous losses on both sides. The enemy made further attacks on the Latvian capital and shifted its focal point to the Dobele area to the west. The units of the 11th *SS* Armored Grenadier Division "Nordland" that went along were pulled out of their attained positions just before Baldone and assembled in the Tukkum area via Riga and Riga-Strand. From there the *SS* members marched through Jaunapils into the now-threatened Dobele area. A former member of the 11th *SS* Volunteer Armored Grenadier Division "Nordland" remembers the action in Latvia:

"On September 20, 1944, we still had close combat with Soviet troops near Rakke (Estonia). The rumor went around that we would be transferred to Germany—everything was flowing to Germany. Civilians packed their bags and fled. We marched via Tori to Vilyandi. It was now said that we should go to the harbor of Pärnu. Instead we went to Halista and Moiseküla. That was the crossing point from Estonia to Latvia.

Two days later we settled down in a forest near Rujema. On September 23, 1944, we received orders to transfer to the Burtniki Lake via Valmiera. There we had heavy close combat the next day. We mined all the roads, and our artillery shot such heavy fire that even we pulled back abruptly. We could no longer reach Valmiera, but only head for the coast via Limbazi. There we finally settled down. The SS *Engineer Battalion was unloaded, and we went on through Riga and Riga-Strand toward Dobele...."*

On September 28, 1944, the 11th *SS* Volunteer Armored Grenadier Division "Nordland," along with the 4th *SS* Volunteer Armored Grenadier Brigade "Nederland," replaced units of the *Wehrmacht*, which had meanwhile moved back north and west of Dobele. When on October 5, 1944, the 1st Baltic Front (General of the Army Bagramian) attacked the 3rd Armored Army to the south, Army Group North ordered the transfer of several units into the hotly contested area. Among others, the Armored Grenadier Division "Grossdeutschland" and the 5th Armored Division, which had been kept in reserve, were taken out of the HKL around Auce from the "Grasser" Army Battalion.[74] The war diary of the 4th *SS* Volunteer Grenadier Brigade "Nederland" records:

*"Strong enemy attack near Schaulen requires immediate replacing of the 'Grossdeutschland' Fusilier Regiment. 'Nordland' Division immediately replaces regimental staff and regimental units of Armored Grenadier Regiment 24, and thus takes over the two left battalion sectors of the 'Nederland' Brigade on the night of 5-6 October. The Division also brings II./*SS *Armored Grenadier Regiment 24 to the 'Nederland' Brigade on 5 October, so that the Battalion can take over a battalion sector of the 'Grossdeutschland' Fusilier Regiment that night...."*

74. See Appendix 9.

For giving up the II./*SS* Armored Grenadier Regiment 24 "Danmark," the III./ Weapon Grenadier Regiment of *SS* 34[75] (Latvian No. 3) was subordinated to the 11th *SS* Volunteer Armored Grenadier Division "Nordland" at this time. Since the Red Army's troop concentrations suggested a wide attack focal point near Libau, the III. (Germanic) *SS* Armored Corps was alarmed for action in that area. On October 12, 1944, the first units, including the *SS* Flak Battalion 11, were ordered to the area south and southeast of Libau. But they could not prevent the Red Army from reaching the Baltic at Polangen between Memel and Libau two days later, and enclosing Army Group North. To prevent the seriously threatened German front from being overrun and, if possible, achieve a breakthrough to East Prussia along with the I. Army Corps—planned Operation "Geier"—the commander of Army Group North, Senior General Schörner, ordered the transfer of the entire III. (Germanic) *SS* Armored Corps into this area. Schörner wanted thus to give up Courland. But Hitler ordered this bridgehead to be held as a starting point for large offensives to regain the initiative and hold back strong enemy bands.

Coming through Frauenburg, the troops of the 11th *SS* Armored Grenadier Division "Nordland" finally replaced hard-hit *Wehrmacht* battle groups in the Priekule area. The II./*SS* Armored Grenadier Regiment 23 "Norge" (*SS Hauptsturmführer* Bachmeier) took positions north of the Priekule-Vainode rail line on October 15, 1944. The III. Battalion (*SS Hauptsturmführer* Hoffmann) was south of it, as far as Klein Trekni. Here the II./*SS* Armored Grenadier Regiment 24 "Danmark" (*SS Hauptsturmführer* im Masche) joined them. Its III. Battalion (*SS Sturmbannführer* Kappus) followed from Grudelis to the swamp southeast of Purmsati. The Division's command post was in Mai, on the Priekule-Libau road.

The first battle of Courland began the very next day. One focal point was on the left wing of the 16th Army, and the other on the right wing of the 18th Army. Here the power of the offensive met the 11th *SS* Volunteer Armored Grenadier Division "Nordland" and the 30th Infantry Division to its left. When the Red Army succeeded in breaking a hole between the *SS* Armored Grenadier Regiment 23 "Norge" and its left neighbor, a regiment of the 30th Infantry Division, parts of the 4th Armored Division moved up to close them. The *SS* Armored Grenadier Regiment 24 "Danmark" on the division's right wing was also hit hard. The 11th *SS* Volunteer Armored Grenadier Division "Nordland" was then reinforced from the 4th *SS* Volunteer Armored Grenadier Brigade "Nederland." The Brigade's war diary describes this:

75. The Battalion was briefly transferred from the 19th Weapon-Grenadier Division of the *SS* (Latvian No. 2).

The *SS* Volunteer Armored Grenadier Division in Latvia
(September 23, 1944-January 28, 1945)

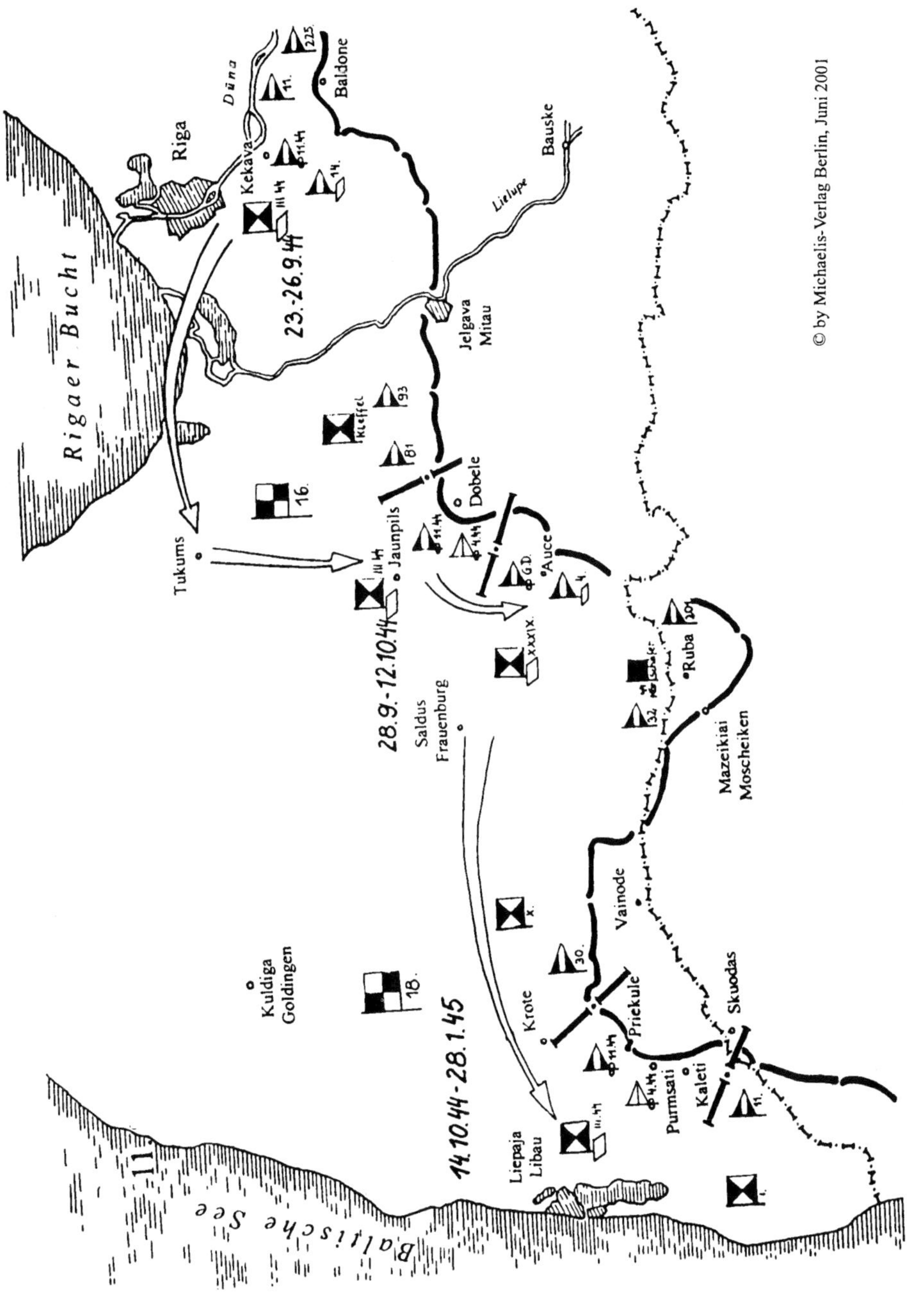

"The Brigade led one battalion of SS *Armored Grenadier Regiment 49 to the command post of* SS *Armored Grenadier Regiment 23 for the use of* SS *Armored Grenadier Regiment 23 until 7:00 on 17 October. Relieved by Ordnance Officer, 'Nordland' Division. All dispensable heavy weapons of the Brigade are to be taken to the 'Nordland' Division effective immediately, and to be used by it in the sector of* SS *Armored Grenadier Regiment 24.* SS *Artillery Regiment 54 is immediately subordinated to AA Artillery Regiment 11 and is to be used by 'Nordland' Division in its right sector..."*

With their greatest exertions, the *SS* members were able to hold their positions. At first the fighting wound down, until on October 27, 1944, the Soviet troops, after unbelievable drumfire, made another attempt to break through the positions. The second Courland battle had begun. The 11th *SS* Volunteer Armored Grenadier Division "Nordland" had more troops sent to them; among others, the *SS* Engineer Battalion 54 was subordinated to the *SS* Armored Grenadier Regiment 24 "Danmark."[76] On the next day the 5th Guard Armored Army (Marshal Romistrov), with heavy artillery, grenade-launcher, and salvo gun support on both sides of the Zarini-Purmsati road, was able to break deeply into the positions of the *SS* Armored Grenadier Regiment 24 "Danmark." Since counterattacks were unsuccessful—for lack of forces—the HKL had to be withdrawn. When enemy troops also broke through between the 4th *SS* Armored Grenadier Brigade "Nederland" and the 11th Infantry Division on October 29, 1944, the *SS* Armored Reconnaissance Battalion 11 was alarmed and, in the night before the next day, cleared up the situation, along with parts of the 11th Infantry Division. After the Red Army shifted their attacks at the beginning of November 1944, the front before the III. (Germanic) *SS* Armored Corps quieted down.

The troops began to build up their positions and were reorganized. While the *SS* Armored Reconnaissance Battalion 11 returned to the Division, the tank- and gunless parts of *SS* Armored Battalion 11 "Hermann von Salza" (*SS Obersturmbannführer* Kausch) and the *SS* Assault Gun Battalion 11—renamed *SS* Tank Destroyer Battalion 11 in September 1944 (*SS Sturmbannführer* Schulz-Streeck)—left Courland to take on new weapons and equipment in Germany.[77] At the end of November 1944, the fighting before the front of the

76. The *SS* Engineer Battalion 54 stayed with the Division until November 15, 1944, and was then ordered back to the *SS* Armored Grenadier Brigade "Nederland."

77. The *SS* Armored Battalion 11 went first to Gotenhafen, and was then brought to full strength in Landeck (Pomerania). At the end of January 1945 the Battalion, still without tanks, was briefly at the Grafenwöhr troop training camp, but was soon ordered to Stettin. There the Armored Battalion received 30 assault guns and 30 Panzer V tanks.

The *SS* Tank Destroyer Battalion 11 was also sent to Germany by ship, and marched to the *SS* troop training camp at Neuhammer. At the end of January 1945 it was ordered to join Army Group "Weichsel" in the Deutsch-Krone area.

11th *SS* Volunteer Armored Grenadier Division "Nordland" flared up briefly. The then *SS* Rottenführer Albert Sudhoff recalls:

"*When I walked around a shed, I was suddenly standing in front of a T-34 that was pointing—or so it seemed—its gun at me. Frightened, I fired my* Panzerfaust *and rushed into the shed. Outside there was a tremendous noise, and I landed in the midst of guys. At first I could not see clearly, but I felt a sword-belt and a sidearm. I groped farther and felt a sticky mass on my hands. It took a short time before I understood that comrades had gone into hiding before me and had not survived a direct hit.*

I felt that I was at the low point of a terrible depression. Outside there was noise, and smoke and stink came into the shed, spreading a sweetish smell. I wanted to get myself out of the smoke, but two Russians appeared at the door. I suddenly threw myself beside my comrades and played dead. Then the Ivans shot blindly into the heap and disappeared. A pistol shot had struck me in the upper thigh, and my leg went its own way and shook around.

Then suddenly two SPW and a Sanka of ours were outside. The comrades came in and carried some men outside. I was unnoticed, and my hollering was presumably not heard. The vehicles moved on, and I crawled out of the shed as best I could. The Sanka was filled to the roof with wounded men, and about 100 meters away from me—then it took a direct hit, and I saw with horror how the bodies flew through the air...."

When the third battle of Courland began on December 21, 1944, things stayed quiet in the area of the III. (Germanic) *SS* Armored Corps except for light enemy fire. A month later the II./*SS* Volunteer Armored Grenadier Regiment 23 "Norge" was gathered in the area west of Kaleti as a corps reserve. The III. Battalion was north of Priekule. The II./*SS* Volunteer Armored grenadier Regiment 24 "Danmark" was on the front north of Purmsati; the III. Battalion south of Priekule. The *SS* Armored Reconnaissance Battalion 11 covered the area south of Purmsati. The *SS* Battalion z.b.V. "Nordland," used since its establishment with the 4th *SS* Volunteer Armored Grenadier Brigade "Nederland," came back to the Division and was active before Purmsati.[78] The then *SS Unterscharführer* Edi Janke remembers the 3rd battle of Courland:

"*One day in December 1944 a heavy snowstorm began. I informed the whole platoon that the Russians could come in white camouflage, and they should all be especially watchful. In the evening I lay down, but was awakened by the shout of one of the machine-gunners:* 'Unterscharführer, *the Russians are here.' I sprang up and took my flare pistol. As I fired a white flare, some 30 Red Army men stiffened at once. Immediately I shot off a*

78. See chapter: The *SS* Battalion z.b.V. "Nordland" in the 4th *SS* Volunteer Armored Grenadier Brigade "Nederland."

second flare. Then the machine-gunner at right swung his gun around and fired a whole belt into the pack. When I fired a third flare, we saw the Russians running away. At the end we found one injured and nine dead Russians, who had broken through our wires and had just planted a mine before us. I made a report, and the company chief gave the alert machine-gunner his own EK I. The name of the gunner: SS Sturmmann *Konrad.*"

On January 23, 1945, the Red Army opened the 4th battle of Courland with Priekule as the focal point. The main assault hit the right flank of the 30th Infantry Division, the III./*SS* Armored Grenadier Battalion 23 "Norge," and both battalions of the sister regiment "Danmark." The Soviet units were able to roll over the II./*SS* Armored Grenadier Regiment "Danmark," among others, and break deep into the German positions. On January 25, 1945, the 14th Armored Division began a counterattack in the Kaleti-Purmsati area, and was able to win back the old HKL by evening. The enemy saw no chance of getting anywhere here, and moved his attack southward to the 4th *SS* volunteer Armored Grenadier Brigade "Nederland." Here, too, the 14th Armored Division provided support. Two days later, when the 4th battle of Courland ended, they already had orders to take all units of the III. (Germanic) *SS* Armored Corps out of the front and prepare for transport by sea to Germany. At the end of January 1945 the X. Army Corps took over the positions of the withdrawing *SS* units. Heinz Gensow remembers the last days in Priekule:

"*Our command post was in the cellar of a school. It often seemed like a beehive. One conference of the company leader followed another. The 3rd and 4th Companies were in front of the school and to the left behind the freight station. There was much open land there, and the Russians had good ideas. They took a shot at anyone who showed himself. As a messenger, I had covered the path several times and also sought cover between the rails. I will remember the day when* SS Sturmbannführer *Saalbach said to me after a telephone call: 'Young fellow, you are the first to know. We are being taken from Courland to Germany at the end of January.'*"

Another former division member writes:

"*When two comrades came from the supply train on January 23, 1945, they told us that parts of the III. (Germanic)* SS *Armored Corps were embarking from Libau! Four days later, we also drove out of the fire zone and landed in Libau on 29 January. On the next day we were all on the 'Karin von Bornhofen,' and fortunately had a quiet voyage to Stettin.*"

SS Armored Grenadiers in a trench, Courland, January 1945.

Sea transport from Libau to Stettin, February 1945.

The Fighting in Pomerania

On January 12, 1945, the Soviet winter offensive had begun. In three days the Red Army pushed forward to the west from several bridgeheads on both sides of Warsaw with a width of 400 kilometers. Upper Silesia was rolled over and East Prussia threatened with being cut off. The introduction of the 6th (*SS*) Armored Army from the west promoted by the German military command, and of Army Group "Kurland" at a *de facto* lost position, to Pomerania were refused by Hitler. Beginning on January 21, 1945, Army Group "Weichesl" (Vistula) was formed in a rush. *Reichsführer-SS* Himmler, named as Commander of the new army group on 25 January, arrived in Deutsch-Krone on his command train "Steiermark," and was to close the shattered front between Glogau and Elbing. Between the 9th Army and Army Group Weichsel was a gap of 150 kilometers.

The 1st White Russian Front (Marshal Zhukov) went along the Netze and Warthe toward Berlin and, after reaching the Oder between Frankfurt and Küstrin on January 30, 1945, made new attacks. Although the possibility of crossing the Oder at once had existed, Marshal Zhukov did not do so—supply difficulties and increasing lack of discipline in the Red Army were the reasons. The Konitz-Ratzebuhr-Deutsch Krone-Pyritz line to the Oder opposite Schwedt formed the front in Pomerania early in February 1945.

While the White Russian Front had come directly to the Oder, the 2nd White Russian Front (Marshal Rokosovsky) had the task of occupying Pomerania and ruling out the danger of a German attack on the right flank of the 1st White Russian Front, which was advancing far to the west. Such an attack in the enemy's flank had been suggested by the Chief of the Army General Staff, Senior General Guderian, as a great solution after the 6th (*SS*) Armored Army had been brought in from the west.[79] But Hitler refused, saying that the use of that army to relieve Budapest was a higher priority. Thus, a smaller solution was worked out in the next few days, and as of January 26, 1945, the 11th Army was formed anew from the staff of the "Oberrhein" Command. On the same day, the High Command of Army Group Weichsel moved northwestward 42 km toward Falkenburg. *SS Obergruppenführer* and General of the *Waffen-SS* Steiner was given the command of the new 11th Army on January 28, 1945.

79. Guderian's plans looked as follows: Two armored corps would push forward to the south from the area southeast of Stettin to stop the Soviet advance to the Oder and give German forces west of the Oder time to set up defenses on the Oder. Besides that, the German units along the Baltic Sea to Danzig were to be given the chance to organize and, if possible, begin an orderly withdrawal. From the Guben-Glogau area, German troops should also move in a northeasterly direction and, if possible, make contact with the northern group.

Lieutenant General Unrein[80] took command of the III. (Germanic) *SS* Armored Corps which, along with the so-called "Walküre" or "Gneisenau" units (replacement and training troops, home guards, etc.), was subordinated to the 11th Army. On February 4, 1945, the situation book of Army Group Weichsel recorded:

"*Of the III.* SS *Corps, 1.3 are now unloaded in Stettin, 1/3 is about to be unloaded.*"

The AOK 11 (about 80,000 men) took command, from the mouth of the Finow Canal in the Oder to the Jastrow-Ratzebuhr-Neustettin line, over:

- the Army Corps "Pommern" (later renamed "Oder")
- the Deputy General Command of the 2nd Army Corps (later renamed "Hörnlein" Army Corps)
- the newly formed X. *SS* Army Corps (*SS Obergruppenführer* and General of the *Waffen-SS* and Police von dem Bach)
- the Corps Group "von Tettau"
- the III. (Germanic) *SS* Armored Corps (Lieutenant General Unrein)

On February 5, 1945, the situation book of Army Group Weichsel recorded that about half of the III. (Germanic) *SS* Armored Corps was unloaded at Stettin. The headquarters of AOK 11 moved from Croessinsee to Plathe on that day. Even before the III. (Germanic) *SS* Armored Corps was completely assembled, the two units of the 11th *SS* Volunteer Armored Grenadier Division "Nordland," and the heavy *SS* Armored Battalion 503 subordinate to it, were already in their first battles in Pomerania.

First Battle Groups in Action

The *SS* Tank Destroyer Battalion 11 (withdrawn from Courland in November 1944), under the command of *SS Sturmbannführer* Schulz-Streeck, came from the *SS* troop training camp at Neuhammer with some 800 men and 29 assault guns, plus 12 antitank guns,[81] and reached Deutsch-Krone (some 63 km east of Reetz) at the end of January 1945. Along with an assault-gun battalion of the Army, an engineer unit, and a battalion (Major Hörl) of Paratroop Regiment 25 (Major Schacht) of the 9th Paratroop Division, it formed the Battle Group "Schulz-Streeck" and was subordinated to the X. *SS* Army Corps (commanded since February 10, 1945, by Lieutenant General Krappe).[82]

The 1./*SS* Tank Destroyer Battalion 11 (*SS Obersturmführer* von Rentelen) marched with parts of the Paratroop Battalion "Hörl" on February 4, 1945, from Kallies to Nantikow,

80. See Appendix 9.
81. The numbers divide into two assault-gun batteries with 14 and 15 assault guns, plus an antitank company with twelve 7.5 cm antitank guns.
82. See Appendix 9.

which could be occupied, along with Hassendorf, after a short fight. Four days later the Red Army was able to enclose the German troops at Nantikow in a counterattack. Since *SS Sturmbannführer* Dr. Schulz-Streeck was out of action with his lower jaw broken by a shot plus a broken left wrist, *SS Obersturmbannführer* Kausch,[83] advancing from Reetz with his *SS* Armored Battalion 11 "Hermann von Salza," took command of the German troops in action there. The enclosed troops broke loose and made contact with the German HKL beyond the Ihna. In March 1945 the *SS* Tank Destroyer Battalion 11 was removed from its subordination to the X. *SS* Army Corps and went back to the III. (Germanic) *SS* Armored Corps.

The *SS* Armored Battalion 11, with a strength of 30 assault guns and 30 Panzer V tanks, reached the readiness area of the III. (Germanic) *SS* Armored Corps early in February 1945, and was first ordered to the Jakobsdorf-Kleinsilber-Glambeck area to secure the gathering of the corps, along with the II./*SS* Armored Grenadier Regiment 23 "Norge." In the night of February 6, 1945, one company secured Zachan with 15 assault guns. There were fights with advancing Soviet troops.

Parts of *SS* Armored Battalion 11 received orders to advance to Arnswalde and reinforce the newly arrived *SS* Escort Battalion "*Reichsführer-SS*" (*SS Sturmbannführer* Gross) in the fighting around Schönwerder. After taking the town quickly, the companies of *SS* Armored Battalion 11 moved on to Reetz. The II./*SS* Armored Grenadier Regiment 23, which was directed to Altenwedell, was already there. At Reetz, the enemy formed an offensive focal point heading toward Nörenberg. The Russians were able to take Reetz on February 7, 1945. The *SS* Armored Battalion 11 moved on to Nantikow and made it possible for the German troops enclosed there to break free.

The heavy *SS* Armored Battalion 503 (*SS Obersturmbannführer* Herzig) had been loaded in Lage with its 39 Tiger II tanks on January 26, 1945. Two days later they reached Pomerania and were divided among various troop units. For example, the III. Platoon of the 2nd Company saw action in Schneidemühl, and finally near Küstrin. While parts were subordinated to the Deputy General Command II and were sent to the "Munzel" Corps, other parts were subordinated to the 9th Army. On *Reichsstrasse* 104 individual units marched to Reetz and then southwestward to Arnswalde. On the evening of February 3, 1945, four Tiger II tanks of the 1st Company reached the city. On the next afternoon four more tanks pushed on to occupy the fortress. On February 8, 1945, the parts of *SS* Armored Battalion 503 enclosed in Arnswalde, along with the (furlough) Alarm Battalion "Enge" and parts of light Flak Battalion 83 came into heavy defensive fighting near Schönwerder

83. See Appendix 9.
84. Strength: 5 companies with heavy weapons.

and Sandow. On February 17, 1945, 17 Tigers in the Zachan area, under the command of *SS Obersturmbannführer* Herzig, moved toward Danzig and were subordinated to the XXIII. Army Corps. They took part in fighting at Dirschau, Gnieschau, and finally Danzig.

To prevent another advance from the Reetz area, the *SS* Battle Group "Schäfer" (*SS Obersturmbannführer* Schäfer) was quickly formed of the *SS* Engineer Battalions 11 and 54 ("Nederland"), which had meanwhile arrived in Stettin. They took up favorable defensive positions on the hills beyond the Ihna. The following parts of the III. (Germanic) *SS* Armored Corps were also ordered to that focal point.

The Action of the Division

On February 5, 1945, the III. (Germanic) *SS* Armored Corps took command in the Freienwalde—Neu-Wedell area. Without the possibility of reorganizing the troops, the General Command ordered on February 12, 1945, in view of the coming combat focal point relief of Arnswalde, and immediate refreshing of the two armored grenadier units.[85] The 11th *SS* Volunteer Armored Grenadier Division "Nordland" (strength some 6000 men) was accordingly to be made of:

- Division Staff with map room, Escort Company, and Field Police Company,
- *SS* Armored Grenadier Regiment 23 "Norge" with II. and III. Battalions, at least one battalion motorized,
- *SS* Armored Grenadier Regiment 24 "Danmark," same as Regiment 23,
- *SS* Armored Artillery Regiment 11 with I. and II. Light Battalions (with three batteries of four guns) and III. Heavy battalion (three batteries of heavy howitzers, each with four guns and one battery 10 K 18 with four guns),
- *SS* Armored Engineer Battalion 11 with one assault engineer, one barrage, and one auxiliary and war bridge company,
- *SS* Armored *Jäger* Battalion 11 with three companies,
- *SS* Armored Reconnaissance Battalion 11 with five companies,
- *SS* Intelligence Battalion 11 with two companies,
- *SS* Flak Battalion 11 with three companies,
- *SS* Armored Regiment 11, newly formed staff as command unit for *SS* Armored Battalion 11 "Hermann von Salza" and heavy *SS* Armored Battalion 503.

85. Gen. Kdo. III (Germanic) *SS* Armored Corps, Ia Tgb. No. 263/45 geh. of February 12, 1945.

At the same time, the former *SS* Armored Battalion 11, now the I. Battalion of the new *SS* Armored Regiment 11 in Stettin, received 30 assault guns and 30 Panzer V tanks, and was thus brought to full strength. The II. Battalion—the former heavy *SS* Armored Battalion 503—had 39 Tiger II tanks. Despite the Armored Regiment, the name remained 11th SS Volunteer **Armored Grenadier** Division "Nordland."

On February 14, 1945, the division was alarmed. The war diary of the former 4th *SS* Volunteer Armored Grenadier Brigade "Nederland," known since February 10, 1945, as the 23rd *SS* Volunteer Armored Grenadier Division "Nederland," recorded:

"The situation in Arnswalde makes an attack by the closed 'Nordland' Division on Arnswalde necessary to establish a firm connection."

The next day the German troops in the area south of Stargard—along the Ihna—Reetz—Kallies, prepared to attack in the direction of Berlinchen and Friedeberg. The 11th Army went into the Pomeranian offensive with the code name "Sonnenwende":

- "Hörnlein" Corps with 9th Paratroop Division between the Oder and Madue Lake,
- XXXIX. Armored Corps with "Holstein" Armored Division, 10th *SS* Armored Division "Frundsberg," 4th *SS* Police Armored Grenadier Division and Battle Group 28, and *SS* Volunteer Grenadier Division "Wallonien," between Madue Lake and Ihna,
- III. (Germanic) *SS* Armored Corps with 11th *SS* Volunteer Armored Grenadier Division "Nordland," Battle Group 27, and *SS* Volunteer Grenadier Division "Langemarck." 23rd *SS* Volunteer Armored Grenadier Division "Nederland" and 281st Infantry Division between Ihna and Reetz,
- "Munzel" Armored Corps with *Führer* Escort and *Führer* Grenadier Division to secure flanks at Neu-Wedell and the Drage,
- X. *SS* Army Corps with *SS* Battle Group "Schulz-Streeck," 402nd Division z.b.V. and 5th *Jäger* Division for a concerted attack toward Kallies,
- Corps "von Tettau" z.b.V. with Action Divisions "Baerwalde" and "Koeslin," plus 163rd Infantry Division as left army wing.

On February 16, 1945, the Pomeranian offensive began. Arnswalde became the goal of the 11th *SS* Volunteer Armored Grenadier Division "Nordland." At first light the II./*SS* Armored Grenadier Regiment 24 passed the securing line of the *SS* Battle Group "Langemarck" and formed a bridgehead near Fährzoll. In the subsequent taking of Reichenbach and Bobin the II. and III./*SS* Armored Grenadier Regiment 24 "Danmark," the II./*SS* Armored Grenadier Regiment "Norge," and one battalion of the *SS* Battle Group "Langemarck" were involved. The Battalion of the *SS* Armored Grenadier Regiment "Norge" quickly won a part of Schlagenthin.

On February 17, 1945, the town could be completely taken, and the securing line moved forward to Stolzenfelde and Marienberg. Thus, the east flank of the assault wedge was secured. The western border was protected by the *SS* Armored

Grenadier Regiment 24 "Danmark," along with parts of the *SS* Battle Group "Langemarck," some assault guns of the *SS* Tank Destroyer Battalion 11, and the SPW Battalion of the *Führer* Escort Division. At the same time, the first troops reached Arnswalde. The link with the enclosed city had been made after strong resistance. The evacuation of the ca. 5000 civilians and wounded began at once through a corridor, some two kilometers wide, to the north. The four still usable Tiger II tanks of the II./*SS* Armored Regiment 11 (*SS* Armored Regiment 503) were withdrawn from the city in the course of the transfer order from the city to Danzig via Marienberg and Reichenbach.

During February 18, 1945, it was relatively quiet in the area of the 11th *SS* Volunteer Armored Grenadier Division "Nordland." But the reinforcement of the Soviet units along the Arnswalde-Schönwerder-Doelitz rail line was noticeable. Since the Soviet resistance steadily increased, and counterattacks were made constantly, Army Group "Weichsel" decided, "*in order to avoid the worthless exhausting of the attack units*," to halt the offensive after three days. The situation book of Army Group "Weichsel" recorded on February 20, 1945:

"*Through our own attack from the north, the preparations of the 2nd and 1st (Soviet) Armored Armies were not disturbed, since the enemy threw new forces into the attack against us.*"

Although a large-scale Soviet attack was to be awaited, numerous German units were transferred to other front sectors after the attack was halted. While the final task was prepared in Arnswalde, the *SS* Armored Grenadier Regiment 24 "Danmark" experienced heavy fighting in the Schönwerder area, as did the *SS* Armored Grenadier Regiment 23 "Norge" east of there. The Red Army wanted to surround Arnswalde and the relatively strong German troops fighting there again.

On February 21, 1945, the AOK 11 ordered the 11th *SS* Volunteer Armored Grenadier Division "Nordland" to withdraw from the front curve near Arnswalde to the Ihna. By midnight of 22 February the rear guards—the III./*SS* Atrmored Grenadier Regiment 24 from the outskirts of Bonin and the III./*SS* Armored Grenadier Regiment 23 from Schlagenthin—drew back over the Fährmuehle bridgehead. The II./*SS* Armored Grenadier Regiment 24, located there, blew up the Ihna bridge and gave up the bridgehead.

On February 24, 1945, the *SS* Armored Grenadier Regiment 24 "Danmark" marched out of the Barskewitz-Dahlow area via Stargard to the Lange Berge—Streesen—Faule Ihna line. The II. Battalion was taken out and formed a corps reserve near Freienwalde. On the Ihna front, the AA Battle Group "Wallonien" moved in on both sides of Kremzow. South of Zadelow-Zachan was the rest of the two battalions of the 27th AA Volunteer Grenadier Division "Langemarck." Fahrzoll was held by the *SS* Escort Battalion "*Reichsführer-SS*" and Altenwedel by the *SS* Armored Grenadier Regiment 23 "Norge."

The Fighting in Pomerania

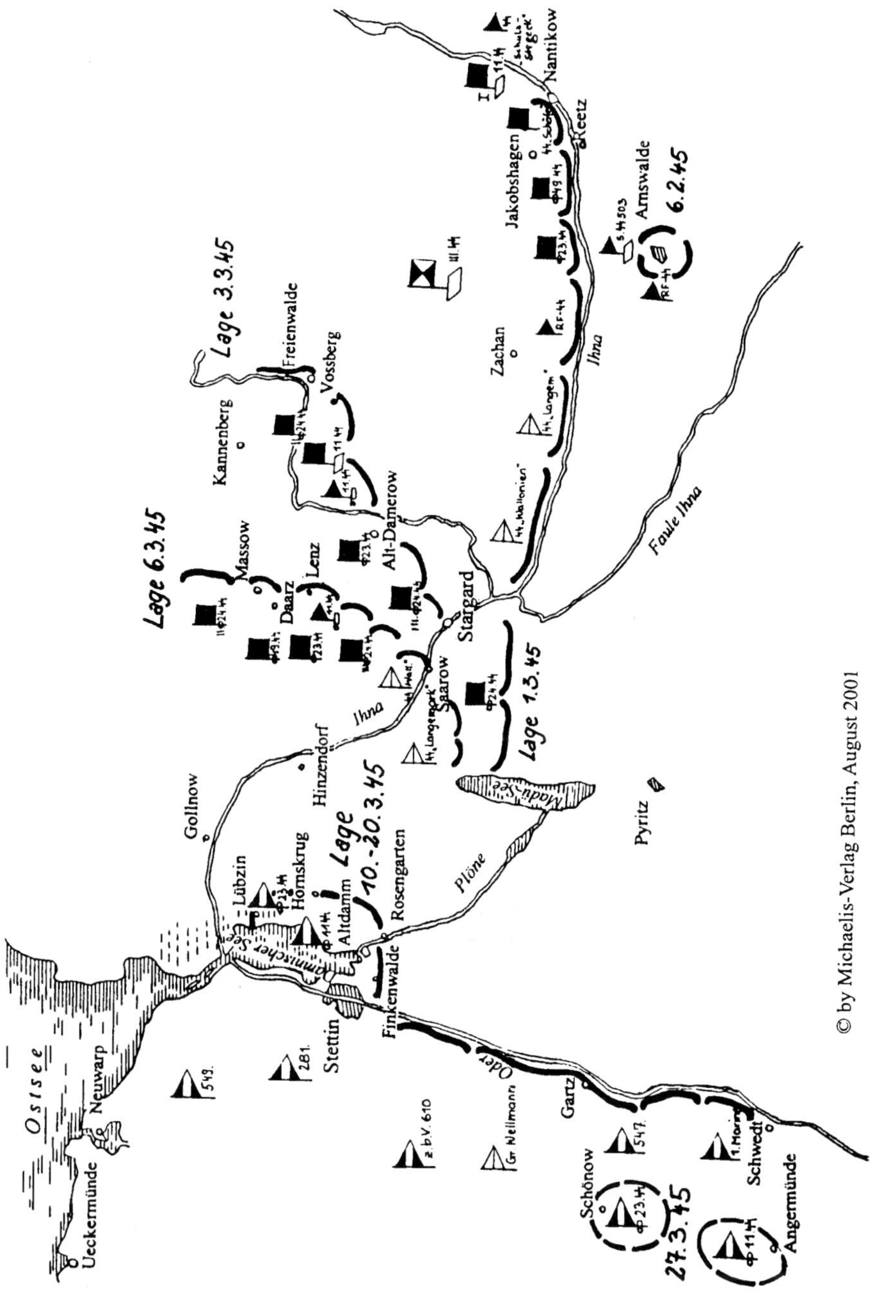

The *SS* Armored Grenadier Regiment 48 was connected with it to Konraden. The 5th *Jäger* Division held Steinberg and was at Hassendorf, as did the *SS* Battle Group "Schulz-Streeck," as already noted. After the AOK moved to the west in March 1945, the Armored AOK 3 took command in the area before Stargard.

When the aforementioned Soviet major offensive along the Ihna began on March 1, 1945, the Red Army made almost the entire German front break down within hours. At Reetz, the enemy troops were able to push forward between the X. *SS* Army Corps and the III. (Germanic) *SS* Armored Corps and finally surround the first corps near Dramburg and shatter them by March 5, 1945.

The III. (Germanic) *SS* Armored Corps had been forced by the fast enemy advance toward the Baltic to move its left wing constantly farther to the northwest. Thus, the HKL already followed the Madue Lake-Freienwalde line on March 2, 1945. The II./*SS* Armored Grenadier Regiment 24 "Danmark" (*SS Sturmbannführer* Sörensen)—as the left flank of the 11th *SS* Armored Grenadier Division "Nordland"—was subordinated to the 23rd *SS* Volunteer Armored Grenadier Division "Nederland," and was finally in heavy fighting northeast of Freienwalde. The *SS* Armored Regiment 11[86] followed to the southwest and was supposed to smash enemy troops in the Vossberg area again. The *SS* Armored Reconnaissance Battalion 11 and the *SS* Armored Grenadier Regiment 23 joined them southwest of Dahlow. The right flank was formed by the III./*SS* Armored Grenadier Regiment 24. *SS Unterscharführer* Edi Janke remembers:

"When the Russians had broken through on March 1, 1945, we usually held a village for 24 hours during the withdrawal, and then came the order: 'Back to the next village.' First came the enemy tanks; we ourselves usually had just one antitank gun, which was set up behind a hill and shot down the first tank. Then the tanks stopped and sent the infantry forward. The infantry was beaten down by us—many times they tried it again. Then it got dark and we received the order to move back to the next village. In this type of defense we had few losses.

Once a King Tiger was subordinated to us. As the heavy fighting eased up in the next village and it became completely quiet, I got the order to drive my SPW into the village and look to the right. As I set off with my crew, I had to go through a patch of woods between the two villages. A lieutenant of the Wehrmacht *stopped us in the woods. Since he had just come here from the workshop with his tank, he wanted to know where the front was. I told him what I was doing, and he wanted to wait for my return. I did not need to drive into the*

86. The Regiment consisted of what was left of the *SS* Armored Battalion 11 and half of the heavy *SS* Armored Battalion 503 as the II. Battalion.

village, for I saw from afar through my telescope that the village was full of Russians. Now we drove back. As I informed the lieutenant, we suddenly heard tank noise coming nearer and nearer. I ran back to the next curve, and there I saw already that several tanks were approaching us. The first tank must have seen me, for they all stopped suddenly. We drove back to our village at top speed, and I reported to the company leader that the tanks were already moving toward our village. The tank commander—a Knight's Cross bearer—was obviously happy about the visit of the Russian tanks. I was to inform our Pak *that they should not fire first under any conditions. The King Tiger went toward the enemy tanks and took a position behind a hill. Finally the first Russian tanks came out of the woods. But the King Tiger did not fire. We all felt uneasy. Only as the 13th tank left the woods did he soot down the last one, and our* Pak *then shot down the first. Now the enemy was all mixed up. They tried to turn, but the King Tiger was faster. He shot down the 12th, 11th, etc. In half an hour the last Russian tank was burning, without any of them having fired a shot.*

On March 8, 1945, we were beside a big road that was lined on both sides with thick poplars. Our Pak *had already shot down the first enemy tank. I myself was lying behind a thick tree when an* SS Untersturmführer *came up to me from behind. He had once fallen out of favor in Courland—but his greeting was very hearty, and he told me that he had come to shoot down an enemy tank with a* Panzerfaust. *I replied that I had already tried it myself, but nothing could be done. He went off all the same, but soon came back. There was really nothing to be done. So we sat there and talked. Suddenly there was noise; a tank had fired at our poplar. The* SS Untersturmführer *shouted that he had several splinters. We took him to the dressing station. There he died the same evening...."*

SS Sturmmann Heinz Gensow recalls:

"*The city of Jakobshagen was evacuated and a new holding line was to be formed. So our way led through Vossberg, a small village on a rail line. While our commander and the company chiefs gathered to discuss the situation, some of us tried to find something edible in the empty houses or take a little nap. The village lay there as on a Sunday afternoon—the trees were just turning green and everything was really peaceful. My comrades and I looked for a farm and were gathering things when we suddenly met two Russians! We had really not expected to meet Red Army men here. They fired their machine pistols at once and hit one of my comrades in the abdomen. This gave us a shock, and we could not react at all. Thus, the quiet in the village was over, and there was shooting all over the place. On all sides there were Russians, only the rail line and highway underpass were still free. But some enemy T-34 tanks were approaching already.*

But miracles do happen, and suddenly two Tiger tanks [of Armored Regiment 11, author's note] *were there. I don't know where they came from. One took a position behind a barn, the other behind a haystack. They opened fire on the Russian tanks... I think almost every shot hit them. In a short time, several tanks were shot down—the enemy drew back.*

We broke through the highway underpass with our SPWs and reached another village. There we saw that a Russian Pak *wanted to take a position. The car to our left drove straight at the* Pak *and rolled right over it, The Russians ran like mad—but there were always new Red Army men. At the edge of town we met fleeing people and took some of them along. I was wounded by a splinter on the upper thigh as we drove through, and finally reached the dressing station with a* Sanka."

While the two cornerstones, Freienwalde and Stargard, could be held—the latter by Walloon *SS* volunteers—the front between them broke down. The III. (Germanic) *SS* Armored Corps ordered a return to the Massow-Stargard line. Then the II./*SS* Armored Grenadier Regiment 24 "Danmark" moved out of its positions to Kannenberg on the night of March 4, 1945. Further heavy fighting followed there, along with the *SS* Battle Group "Kausch" (what remained of *SS* Armored Regiment 11) and parts of Paratroop Regiment 25.

The *SS* Armored Reconnaissance Battalion 11 saw action near Alt-Damerow, as did the three remaining battalions of the two armored grenadier regiments on the Kietzig-Buchholz line. Fighting followed for *SS* Armored Grenadier Regiment 23 "Norge," along with *SS* Armored Reconnaissance Battalion 11, near Parlin and Lenz. While the II. Battalion was still fighting in the area of the 23rd *SS* Volunteer Armored Grenadier Division "Nederland" near Reschl, the III./*SS* Armored Grenadier Regiment 24 "Danmark" was in the field before Mulkenthin.

On March 5, 1945, Himmler—obviously completely unaware of the actual situation and events—sent a message about the counterattack of *SS* Armored Regiment 11 in the Vossberg area to the Commanding General of the III. (Germanic) *SS* Armored Corps, Lieutenant General Unrein:

"*I hear that Nordland has attacked and fought well. Fight through with the strongest means. I expect that Nordland will do its duty as before.*"

Constantly in motion, the 11th *SS* Volunteer Armored Grenadier Division "Nordland," via Wachlin, Hinzendorf, and Hornskrug, reached the area around Altdamm, foreseen as a bridghehead, on March 7-8, 1945. The northern part (from Lübzin to Hornskrug) was finally defended by the 23rd *SS* Volunteer Armored Grenadier Division "Nederland." Subordinated to it were the II./ *SS* Armored Grenadier Regiment 24 "Danmark," plus parts of the 10th *SS* Armored Division "Frundsberg" and Army units. To the south was the 11th *SS* Volunteer Armored Grenadier Division "Nordland" with *SS* Armored Reconnaissance Battalion 11 and *SS* Armored Grenadier Regiment 23 "Norge" on the Hornskrug-Highway line, and the III./*SS* Armored Gnenadier Regiment 24 "Danmark," *SS* Engineer Battalion 11, and *SS* Flak Battalion 11 to Rosengarten. To the right, near Hökendorf, was the XXXII. Army Corps with what remained of the battle groups of the 27th and 28th *SS* Volunteer Grenadier Divisions "Langemarck" and "Wallonien." The Danish *SS Untersturmführer* Mogens Schwartz reports on the first days of March:

"At the beginning of March 1945 I was to take over a company. I was given maps, and a soldier who appeared by chance was to drive me. Unfortunately, when we arrived, the positions were no longer occupied. So we set off first to the left, but did not see a human soul far and wide. When we wanted to cross a small bridge, we were instantly fired on by Russian infantry. I myself got over the bridge unharmed—my escort thought he had no chance and went back alone. Since it was impossible for me to get back across the bridge unseen, I went farther in search of my company.

I was wearing an old motorcycle coat—the soldier had worn the steel helmet and carried my machine pistol. So I had only a 6.35 mm pistol and a hand grenade. Suddenly three Russian soldiers came toward me and talked to me. Naturally, I understood nothing and patted a Russian amiably on the shoulder. From about 100 meters they called to me again. I jumped over a ditch and found cover behind a single tree. After they had fired but not hit me, I saw them deciding what to do. I took my hand grenade and threw it among the Russians, who were only about 10 meters from me. Then I jumped up quickly and ran over the open field to the edge of the woods. There I found a small pond, at which I hid under a footbridge. I waited there soaking wet until it got dark, and then I went on in my dripping wet clothes. Fortunately I found our troops and heard Norwegian voices. I called, relieved: 'Same troop, don't shoot!' and when I heard the answer 'Understood,' I stepped over the HKL. I was brought to the command post on a tank. I lay on the warm motor hood and soon was dry. At the command post they had already wondered where I was."

Then *SS Obersturmführer* Lorenz writes:

"On March 8, 1945, I finally got the order to march and, despite all the bomb attacks, reached my unit on 11 March. It was at the Altdamm bridgehead with the task of defending to the north, toward Mönchskrug. The Führer *of the 2nd Company, because of constant changes in the front, had gone out beyond his own lines and landed amid the Russians.*

I had almost suffered the same fate. Despite sharpshooters' fire, I reached the command post safely, driving 400 meters to the HKL. Here I met SS Sturmbannführer *Pätsch for the last time, with whom I had been OO and Adjutant. Because of the unit's hard fighting in Courland and east of Stettin in the Stargard area, the unit was very reduced in personnel and vehicles. There were only a few officers there, and the men had changed very much through losses and replacements. I became Chief of the 1st and 2nd companies. After two days we were sent back just behind the front as a mobile attack reserve. The 1st Company consisted of two eight-wheel and two four-wheel armored scout cars, the 2nd Company of some eight armored personnel carriers. The Altdamm bridgehead lasted three more days. Then it was evacuated under very heavy fire.*"

On March 15, 1945, the Red Army went on the offensive again and tried to smash the Altdamm bridgehead. Under steady drumfire, the Commander of the *SS* Volunteer Armored Grenadier Regiment 24 "Danmark," *SS Obersturmbannführer* Krügel, was killed the next day. *SS Hauptsturmführer* Ternedde took command of what remained of the Regiment. Army Group "Weichsel" reported on that day:

"*1. New enemy information lets us know that the enemy is preparing for a decisive attack on Berlin.*

2. The Army Group has therefore postponed its planned attack from the Stettin bridgehead temporarily and is using all means to support the 9th Army's front."

A euphemistic arrangement. The "postponed" attack plan was to push forward from the Altdamm bridgehead in the direction of Danzig—therefore it was absolutely to be held! On March 17, 1945, events overruled this. Army Group "Weichsel" reported gradually:

"*South of Altdamm there is hard fighting on the rail line. On the northeast front, the enemy threw our own units back in numerous attacks on our position 2 km northeast of Altdamm.*"

And:

"*The enemy has pushed past the Altdamm depot on both sides of Reich Route 104. There is the danger that the small groups of the 'Nordland' Division north of Altdamm will be cut off. The Army Group asks that this fact be presented to the* Führer *situation.*"

Hitler reacted just before it was too late. Army Group "Weichsel" informed the 3rd Army:

"*1.* Führer *has approved evacuation of the Stettin bridgehead on the night of 19-20 March.*

2. Pz.AOK 3 is to carry out the transfer from the bridgehead so that the movement of all heavy equipment, especially tanks, artillery, and flak guns, is guaranteed.

3. With the units that become free, the Oder defense near and on both sides of Stettin is to be set up, and the reinforcement of the sector of the Oder Corps and Langenberg bridgehead is to be carried out."

The last parts of the 11th *SS* Volunteer Armored Grenadier Division "Nordland" drew back behind the Oder on the evening of March 20, 1945.

The Final Fighting around Berlin

Along with the remainder of the III. (Germanic) *SS* Armored Corps, the 11th *SS* Volunteer Armored Grenadier Division "Nordland," with a strength of some 4000 men, marched to the area southwest of Stettin. Here the shattered units were to be restructured into an "Armored Division 1945."

According to instructions from the Inspector General of the Armored Troops on March 24, 1945, there was no longer a difference between an armored and an armored grenadier division, but a uniform structure for both was to be introduced.[87] This foresaw two armored grenadier regiments for every two—no longer motorized—battalions, and a mobile battle group of a mixed armored regiment (I. battalion tanks, II. battalion armored grenadier battalion) and one battalion of the armored artillery regiment. In all, the Armored Division 1945 was to have 54 tanks, 22 *Jagdpanzer*, and 90 armored personnel carriers. The 11th *SS* Volunteer Armored Grenadier Division "Nordland" reached a strength of 45 assault guns, several Panzer IV and V tanks, 10 "Hetzer" *Jagdpanzer*, 12 Tiger II tanks, and 78 armored personnel carriers in the next days.

In the course of this restructuring, members of the *Waffen-SS*—including five men of the "British Freecorps"[88] —the *Luftwaffe* and the Navy were ordered to the 11th *SS* Volunteer Armored Grenadier Division "Nordland" to fill out the weak troop units. *SS Obersturmbannführer* Klotz took over the *SS* Armored Grenadier Regiment 24 "Danmark," which had been strengthened by, among others, 100 "tankless" members of *SS* Armored Regiment 11, and now had a strength of some 1500 men. At this time the Division had suffered the following losses during its previous war service (as of September 1, 1943):

	Officers	Other Ranks
Dead	102	2,837
Wounded	267	10,005
Missing	23	1,255

With a total of 14,489 men, this was about the full strength of the Division. In the 1945 combat in Pomerania alone, 366 soldiers died, 1411 were wounded, and 387 men were listed as missing. When on March 26, 1945, the use of the troops as a reserve for the 3rd Armored Army in the Sxchwedt-Freienwalde sector was approved, the Commander of the 3rd Armored Army, General of the Armored Troops von Manteuffel,[89] evaluated the 11th *SS* Volunteer Armored Grenadier Division "Nordland" as follows:

87. Army General Staff/Org. Abt. No. 1/1600/45 g. Kdos. Of March 24, 1945.
88. They went to the 3./*SS* Reconnaissance Battalion 11.
89. See Appendix 9.

"Serious lack of armored grenadiers, lack of officers and NCOs, request should be made of Reichsführer-SS *for hastened personnel filling, good division artillery, excellent reconnaissance battalion (78 armored personnel carriers).*[90] *Tactically subordinated to the Division at this time is half of heavy* SS *Armored Battalion 503 with 6 Panzer VI ready to use, 7 being repaired.*[91] *Division has an excellent fighting spirit and, after personnel and materiel refreshing is carried out, is suitable for any offensive task.*"

On the next day the III. (Germanic) *SS* Armored Corps marched into the area west of Gartz, Schwedt, and Altküstrinchen. At that time, the XXXXVI. Armored Corps was there with the 547th People's Grenadier Division and 1st Naval Division in the HKL. While the 23rd *SS* Volunteer Armored Grenadier Division "Nederland" moved into quarters in the area south of Schönow, the "Nordland" Division Staff took quarters in Altkünkendorf, the *SS* Armored Grenadier Regiment 23 "Norge" near Liepe—not far from the Niederfinow ship hoist—the *SS* Armored Grenadier Regiment 24 "Danmark" was in Landin, and the *SS* Armored Artillery Regiment 11 in Dobberzin.

The Red Army set out from the bridgeheads on the Oder to make the last push between Wriezen and Seelow at the XI. *SS* Army Corps. The 9th Paratroop Division was smashed immediately, and an enemy breakthrough was to be expected. In this situation, the LVI. Armored Corps (General of the Artillery Weidling)[92]—used as a reserve for the 9th Army—was alarmed, along with the 25th Armored Grenadier Division and "Müncheberg" Armored Division. In addition, the Commander of the 9th Army, General of the Infantry Busse,[93] empowered the transfer of the two *SS* Armored grenadier Divisions held in reserve to the north to the area south of Frankfurt an der Oder on April 17, 1945.

During that day the first troop units were sent on the march. Because of transport difficulties—lack of vehicles and fuel—the transfer of the 11th *SS* Volunteer Armored Grenadier Division "Nordland" stopped at first in the area north of Strausberg. Since further transport was not possible in the near future, the Division, contrary to the original command, was to take positions in the Wriezen—Seelow area, and was subordinated to the LVI. Armored Corps. Since the Soviet attack developed into a crisis of the worst kind, General of the Infantry Busse changed his mind and ordered the still-moving 23rd *SS* Volunteer Armored Grenadier Division "Nederland" to stop there as well. Army Group "Weichsel" reported to the OKH on April 18, 1945:

90. With some 15 armored gun cars per company, the 11th *SS* Armored Reconnaissance Battalion 11 had its full strength.
91. Thus, even half the battalion had only about 40% of its full strength. The other "battalion half" was fighting in Danzig and, with four Tiger tanks ready for use, had only the strength of a platoon!
92. See Appendix 9.
93. See Appendix 9.

"9th Army also places 'Nederland' in the main focal point in Seelow-Wriezen area, taking the risk south of Frankfurt in the bargain. Fuel problems in the movements of 'Nord and Nederland.'"

Except for the II./*SS* Armored Grenadier Regiment 24 "Danmark" (*SS Sturmbannführer* Sörensen), which could not be transported from Ladin for lack of possibilities,[94] the rest of the 11th *SS* Volunteer Armored Grenadier Division "Nordland" occupied defensive positions before Strausberg on April 18, 1945. The Division Staff moved into Reichenberg, while the *SS* Armored Regiment 11 along with the *SS* Engineer Battalion 11 was in Reichenow. The III./*SS* Armored Grenadier Regiment 24 "Danmark" (*SS Hauptsturmführer* Ternedde) occupied a line around Batzlow, and the battalions of the sister regiment "Norge" the wood edges south of there, north of Lupinenhof to northwest of Hermersdorf. Here they picked up retreating parts of the shattered 9th Paratroop Division. After initial heavy fighting, the units moved back in the direction of Strausberg on the night of April 19, 1945.

Northwest of the place, the *SS* Engineer Battalion 11 (*SS Sturmbannführer* Voss) secured near Gielsdorf. The *SS* Armored Regiment 11 (*SS Obersturmbannführer* Kausch) fought off a Soviet tank attack near Prötzel (men of the 9th Paratroop Division also fought here). With some 73 tanks in all, the 11th *SS* Volunteer Armored Grenadier Division "Nordland" showed itself to be extraordinarily strong.[95] For shooting down about 100 enemy tanks, Regiment Commander Kausch received the oak leaves to the Knight's Cross on April 23, 1945, the 846th soldier to earn them. South of there, the *SS* Armored Reconnaissance Battalion 11 was fighting near Grunow. The rest of the three armored grenadier battalions followed in the area east of Hohenstein as far as Garzin.

On the night of April 20, 1945, the units unloaded on the Ahrensfelde-Altlandsberg line. Here the members of the 11th *SS* Volunteer Armored Grenadier Division "Nordland" received a wordy document by the *Reichsführer-SS*. But his grandiose words changed nothing in the situation of the German Reich:

94. The battalion could no longer connect with the 11th *SS* Volunteer Armored Grenadier Division "Nordland" and marched with the Army Group "Steiner" (formed from the Staff of the III. (Germanic) *SS* Armored Corps) westward north of Berlin. See also comments at the end of the chapter.

95. In comparison, other *SS* divisions reported much worse figures (as of March 17, 1945):

1. *SS* Armored Division: 14 Panzer IV, 14 Panzer V, 9 Panzer VI (subordinated), and 4 assault guns.
2. *SS* Armored Division: 6 Panzer IV, 8 Panzer V, and 19 assault guns.
3. *SS* Armored Division: 16 Panzer IV, 8 Panzer V, 7 Panzer VI, and 17 assault guns.
4. *SS* Armored Division: 4 Panzer IV, 13 Panzer V, and 8 assault guns.

The Withdrawal of the 11th *SS* Volunteer Armored Grenadier Division "Nordland" to Berlin (April 18-23, 1945)

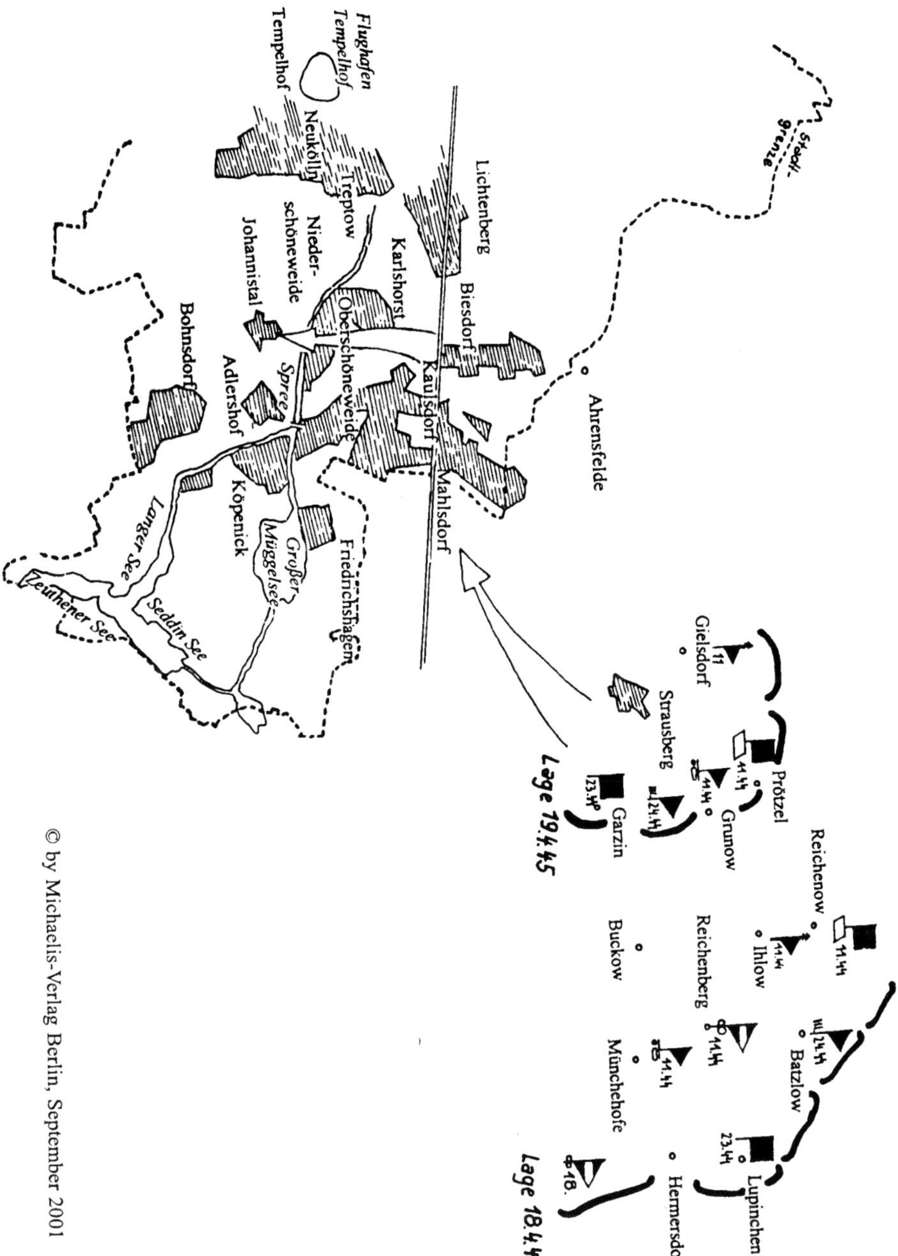

"You stand in the decisive battle in the east. There is no pulling back and getting out. It must be stood to the last man, or it is attacked. The fate of Europe lies in your hands. Think of your dead comrades and of the millions of Germanic women and children. I expect ruthless waging of war and fullest fulfillment of duty."

After the Commanding General of the LVI. Armored Corps, General of the Artillery Weidling, was assigned the defense of the Reich capital by Hitler, he immediately defined the future areas of action of the troops subordinated to him. According to an order by Hitler on March 9, 1945, the city had been divided into an outer and an inner defense ring, as well as nine defensive zones (A to H and Z). The occupiers of the planned defensive sectors remained undone because of the fast and strong advances of the Red Army.

As of the morning of April 22, 1945, the troop units of the 11th *SS* Armored Grenadier Division "Nordland" were already in Mahlsdorf. When the enemy advanced north and south of there, the withdrawal to Biesdorf and, in the evening, to Karlshorst, was ordered. Heinz Gensow remembers:

"The combat alarm became stronger and stronger in the night. The men sat in the houses, some in their tanks, which were also supposed to secure the streets. Toward morning all hell broke loose. The Russians came from Marzahn with tanks and infantry. Within a short time everything was in an uproar. There was a struggle of the small group of our battalion that took up the fight. We could hold back the Russian infantry, and several tanks were shot down. But we had to give way to superior power and withdraw. Now the Russians also came from the Frankfurter Allee, and the way back to the center of the city was cut off. We moved out in an eastern direction via Karlshorst and Schöneweide."

The next day, the very decimated units moved back over the Spree and secured various bridges. The cohesion of the division was completely lost. The rest of the *SS* Armored Reconnaissance Battalion 11 moved to Neukölln as a combat reserve, and the remaining guns of *SS* Artillery Regiment 11 took positions in Britz. The survivors of the III./*SS* Armored Grenadier Regiment 24 held a small bridgehead at the East Cross; to the right, the last platoons of *SS* Engineer Battalion 11 gathered at Treptow Park and Plänterwald. Fragments of *SS* Armored Grenadier Regiment 23 followed in the area of the three bridges in Schöneweide, and the last members of *SS* Flak Battalion 11—mainly engaged in ground combat—were in Adlershof.

On this day the Chief of the General Staff of Army Group "Weichsel" reported to the Pz.A.O.K. 3 that 1100 soldiers of the no longer active 25th *SS* Weapon Grenadier Division "Hunyadi" (Hungarian No. 1) should be brought in from Bavaria;[96] a utopian plan that could only have been carried out by an airlift to Berlin. 500 Hungarian *SS* members were to be subordinated to the 11th *SS* Volunteer Armored Grenadier Division "Nordland." The transfer did not take place.

On April 24, 1945, *SS Hauptstormführer* Ternedde took over what remained of the three armored grenadier battalions, led them to the inner defense ring—Sector C—and formed a line along the S-Bahn ring of Treptow Park—Sonnenallee—Neukölln—Tempelhof. On the right wing, though, Soviet tanks were already driving over the Tempelhof Airport grounds.

Disagreements between General of the Artillery Weidling and *SS Brigadeführer* and Major General of the *Waffen-SS* Ziegler, who did not want to let his men be butchered in Berlin, led on April 25, 1945, to the replacement of the Commander of the 11th *SS* Volunteer Armored Grenadier Division "Nordland." The former commander of the shattered 33rd *SS* Weapon Grenadier Division "Charlemagne" (French No. 1), *SS Brigadeführer* and Major General of the *Waffen-SS* Dr. Krukenberg,[97] took command of the *SS* unit, which now numbered only about 1500 men. Krukenberg brought some 50 French *SS* volunteers[98] along, who fought in the ranks of the 11th *SS* Volunteer Armored Grenadier Division "Nordland" from then on. The *SS Unterscharführer* Burgkart remembers the replacement of Ziegler:

"*On the morning of April 25, 1945, we—*SS Sturmbannführer *Saalbach,* SS Sturmbannführer *Vollmar, and I—stood in front of the stairway entrance to the advanced command post of the Division—a building of the lung hospital in the Hasenheide, and talked. Suddenly we were spoken to from behind: 'Where is the 'Nordland' command post?' I turned around and said: 'Down there in the cellar.' And as I said that, I saw the silver gray coat attachments and knew it was a* Brigadenführer. *He stood behind me, somewhat to the right, at the corner of the building, and then went past me—followed by a couple of* SS *men with machine pistols under their arms—without saying a word.*

When I looked around, I saw that a few trucks carrying SS *men had driven past us, unnoticed. The men got out and formed a chain cutting off the whole street. Everything was stopped. A short time later, we were standing by the cellar entrance, astonished, when* Brigadenführer *Ziegler, with his driver,* Hauptscharführer *Emmert, and his orderly came up the stairs, walked straight up to me, and said 'Burgkart, take your mess kit out of the wagon and, if you have other private belongings, take those too.'*

---

96. Teletype of Army Group "Weichsel" 1a Tgb. No. 5970/45 geh. of April 22, 1945.
97. See Appendix 9.
98. Dr. Krukenberg said in 1979 that there were six tank-destroyer troops, each with an officer and about 15 men. Higher figures—a French assault battalion with 300 and more Frenchmen has been spoken of—do not agree with the facts.

I asked: 'Why that, Brigadenführer*?' The answer: 'Take your things out, I have to go now!'*

Only now did we learn that he was the second SS Brigadenführer*, Dr. Krukenberg of the 33rd Weapon Grenadier Division of the* SS *'Charlemagne,' and the* SS *men with him were French.*

Emmert had meanwhile gotten into the amphibian and had started it. I took my kit, my assault rifle, and overcoat out. Then Ziegler and his orderly got in. He stood in the front of the car, saluted us, and said to the two Sturmbannfiuehrer *standing beside me: 'Gentlemen, all the best!'*

When he was gone, SS Sturmbannführer *Vollmar looked at me and asked: 'What is going on?' And then again: 'What is going on?' I went to take care of some things, and when I wanted to go back to the command post, I was stopped by one of the Frenchmen: 'No, back, no, back!'*

'Hey, who wants to go back?' I shouted. At this moment, in which neither understood the other very well, two or three armored personnel carriers with wounded SS *men drove up. They came from the area south of the Hasenheide. The crews were searching for a hospital for the gasping, groaning, and shrieking comrades. 'Halt, stop, stop,' the Frenchman shouted again. The drivers ignored him and drove on. Suddenly one of the Frenchmen took his assault rifle and shot at the first SPW. The passenger behind the MG-43 reacted by shooting into the bunch of French* SS *men. I saw how three or four Frenchmen were rolling on the ground and yelling. Now I thought, 'get out of here as fast as possible.' With the remainder of the Ia staff, I drove to the new division command post, to the State opera 'Unter den Linden.' There we were divided into groups and settled at the Spittelmarkt.*"

On April 26, 1945, members of the *SS* Volunteer Armored Grenadier Regiment 23 "Norge," along with the French *SS* volunteers, shot down several Soviet tanks in the Hasenheide. After that they had to cross the Landwehrkanal, and on the next day they were at first in the vicinity of the Kottbus Gate. A company-strong *SS* battle group, formed of members of backline units under the command of *SS Untersturmführer* Bachmann, took positions by the Halle Gate. Remainders of *SS* Armored Reconnaissance Battalion 11 defended themselves at the Anhalt Depot. The command posts of the troop fragments were usually in the subway depots along the Frnedrichstrasse. Since the fighting around the German capital began, there was no longer a clear main battle line. The impossibility of viewing the city, the individual streets and buildings, meant that friend and foe recognized each other only when someone shot from some direction or house.

On April 28-29, 1945, the remainder of the *SS* Armored Reconnaissance Battalion 11, along with French volunteers, fought in the area of Potsdam Square, followed by the

The final Battle in Berlin (April 23-May 2, 1945)

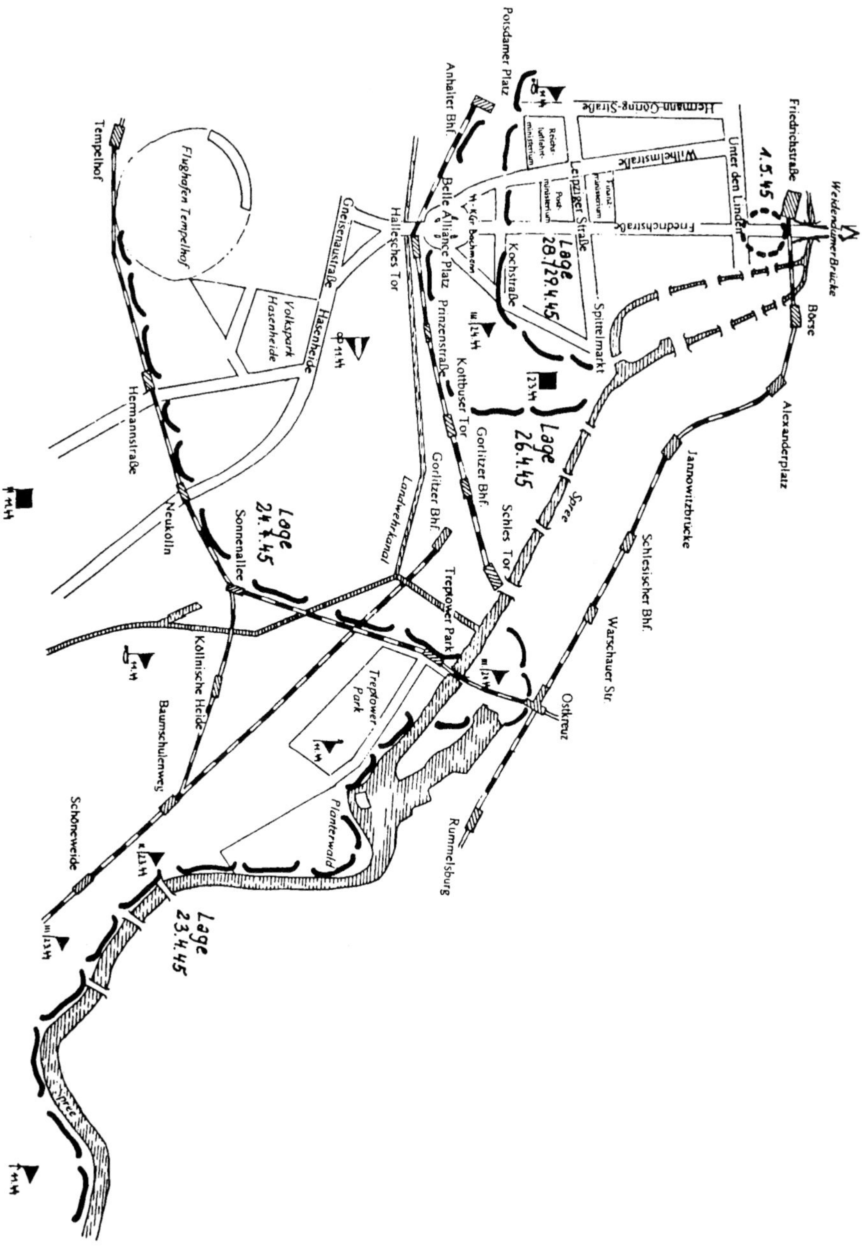

survivors of the III./*SS* Armored Grenadier Regiment 24 "Danmark" in Koch Street and the last of *SS* Armored Grenadier Regiment 23 "Norge" at the Spittelmarkt. While the members of *SS* Engineer Battalion 11 and *SS* Flak Battalion 11—the latter still had some 60 men—were in infantry action, the still-available tracked vehicles of *SS* Armored Regiment 11 (including five Tiger II tanks of heavy *SS* Armored Battalion 11) were in reserve between Leipziger Street and Unter den Linden, and in the Tiergarten.

When Hitler shot himself the next day and the Red Army reached the *Reichstag* building, negotiations for the surrender of Berlin began, as did preparations for the enclosed German troops to break out. The men of the III./*SS* Armored Grenadier Regiment 24 "Danmark" had meanwhile drawn back to the Air Ministry on Leipziger Street, along with the French volunteers and the last of *SS* Armored Reconnaissance Battalion 11. The men of *SS* Armored Grenadier Regiment 23 "Norge" were still east of there in the Spittelmarkt area. A former member recalls:

"*On April 28, 1945, we received an order to take positions at the Prussian State Print Shop. The next day the Russians came nonstop with tanks from the direction of the Halle Gate. The Russian infantry tried to break through with flamethrowers and explosive charges. On 30 April we decided to go back to the Reich Air Ministry about 10:00 PM. Chaos reigned there—nobody knew anything. In the early hours of 1 May we found the supply train on Friedrichstrasse. Since everybody was in a state of hysteria, we—three comrades—separated from the supply train and divided up on 2 May. While the other two went to dressing stations, I went home....*"

The Friedrichstrasse—shortly before the Weidendamm Bridge—became the meeting point for the German troops and civilians who wanted to break through the Soviet positions over the last intact bridge to the north. Shortly after midnight on May 1, 1945, a first group tried it—in vain. About 15 minutes later, a second, likewise failed, attempt was made, supported by a Tiger tank. About 1:00 AM the third attempt began, with support from several armored personnel cars of *SS* Armored Reconnaissance Battalion 11. This attempt also came to grief. There were two more, around 2:00 and 4:00, in which some made it over the bridge to the Stettin Depot but did not come back. The *SS Unterscharführer* Franz Bereznyak remembers:

"*On 29-30 April we were out looking for tanks. There were supposed to be some tank units underway, with which there was no longer any link. They were hellish drives through bombed and burning Berlin, looking for tanks that were no longer there. Unfortunately, we found nothing but one Panzer IV that lay on a street with shot-up tracks and fired wildly into the ruins of several houses.*

What impressed me most were the 12-to-14-year-old Hitler Youth boys who slipped through the ruins with their Panzerfäuste *and shot at Russian tanks. On May 1, 1945, our Chief,* SS Obersturmführer *Pehrsson, said farewell to us with the words: 'Boys, the war is over, save yourselves if you can.'*

Some of us stayed in the cellars to wait, but most of us crossed the Weidendamm Bridge. It was the last hope of getting out of the witch's kettle. It was astonishingly quiet as we reached the bridge, at which a great number of soldiers and civilians had gathered. A few SPW of our battalion were still ready to attack. Toward midnight, a Tiger and an assault gun came along and took the lead of the escapees. The crowd stormed after the Tiger, but only a few were lucky enough to get across the bridge. Most of them were mown down like cornstalks by the Russians who were in the ruins to the left and right across the Spree. The dead piled up on the bridge—I had never seen such a thing in the entire war. The attack stopped when the assault gun was shot down. We drove out of our readiness position and fired all the shells we had in to the ruins on the other side. Then we drove speedily across the bridge. In the hail of bullets we drove as fast as the motor and tracks allowed. When we saw soldiers again and stopped, we noticed that we were at the Stettin Depot. Behind us came another vehicle that had taken a shot in the radiator—the motor was boiling over. Towing it, we drove on in hopes that we had left the worst behind us. Quite wrong—soon I saw Russian tanks on a street and it was all over. A short time later I was captured by two Russians...."

An *SS Untersturmführer* remembers his last war days:

"*An announcement from the Berlin Army Position Commander required all* Wehrmacht *members in Berlin to report to the Seeckt Barracks at once. On the way there—public transport no longer ran—I was stopped by a* Kübelwagen *of the* Waffen-SS *at the Belle-Alliance Square.*

The drivers belonged to the 'Mohnke' Battle Group—including SS Untersturmführer *Bauer, with whom I had been in Ratzeburg with* SS *Tank-Destroyer Replacement Battalion I and at the Panzer School in Janowitz near Prague.*

We drove to the old Reichsbank *and picked up two brand new 5 cm antitank guns. A group of 6-8 men were assigned as gun crews. With one gun we took a position on Leipziger Street—shortly before the Spittelmarkt—and had the task of keeping it free of Russian tanks. Since we had no antitank shells we had to fire delayed-action explosive shells. Behind us in the* Bärenstiefelhaus *was a remainder of 'Charlemagne,' which was moving steadily with flamethrowers. We stood with machine pistols cocked, with our backs to the wall, and waited for the Russians to appear. Then we headed for the assembly point, the Friedrichstrasse subway station. Over rubble, dirt, ruins, and many dead we made our way—many killed themselves. The Russian shells constantly landed in the waiting crowds of people (soldiers and civilians). The attempts to get away were doomed from the start.*

On 2 May the weapons were silent. I strayed through the ruined city and was suddenly facing the Russians. They were not particularly alert and I could disappear. Civilians offered me civilian clothing. The people came cautiously out of the cellars onto the street. On my cautious way toward Tempelhof I was stopped under the elevated in Kreuzberg, because I still wore my military boots under my civilian trousers. But I was able to escape again. Now I moved only at night. In fog and darkness I was able to get to Dabendorf, near Zossen. There I could live unnoticed until May 19, 1945. Captured through denunciation, I landed in various cellars for endless questioning and beating. Via Rüdersdorf, Posen, and Estonia I ended up in Rostov on the Don and was released from imprisonment on January 15, 1950."

The II./*SS* Armored Grenadier Regiment 24 "Danmark" (*SS Obersturmführer* Rasmussen), which had remained in Landin on April 18, 1945, because of transport problems, was integrated into Army Group "Steiner" along with various backline units and moved westward north of Berlin at the end of April 1945. *SS Unterscharführer* Balint remembers:

"*We were on a farm by Benzrode, could rest a bit, and our vehicles were also overhauled. Then we moved back through Mecklenburg, spate a short time in Joachimsthal near Berlin, and finally came to the Elbe. The Americans were already on the other side, but they only came over during the day to look at us; toward evening they went away. And the Russians came closer and closer—one day a Russian commissar came riding up and declared us Russian prisoners of war. He spoke a very passable German and then rode away without bothering about us anymore.*

We made our still operable vehicles useless—but how could we cross the Elbe? One day an Untersturmführer *came with a food truck and wanted to get his whole motor pool across the river. We thought about how we could do it, and removed the truck tires, took out the inner tubes, pumped them up, and built a raft. The* Untersturmführer *did not want to wait, grabbed a tube, and tried to cross the Elbe. He was shot by the Americans...*

We set out on the raft on a foggy night, after our last pay had been given out. The sutler's goods were also divided up. The last words of our Chief, SS Hauptsturmführer *Paul Nieft, were:*

'Comrades, go as well as you can and try to come through somewhere. Some day we'll see each other again on the Lüneburg Heath.'

Nieft kept his word—of course it took 40 years before we saw each other again."

Heinz Gensow

Memorial stone bear Prötzel.

A shot-down assault gun in front of the Reich Chancellery in 1945.

Voss Street and the Chancellery, June 1945.

The new Reich Chancellery, circa 1946.

The I. Battalions of *SS* Armored Grenadier Regiments 23 and 24 in the IV. *SS* Armored Corps

After the two first battalions of *SS* Armored Grenadier Regiments 23 and 24 had been shattered in the heavy withdrawal fighting from the Oranienbaum pocket to Narva, the survivors were divided among the other battalions. At the end of April 1944 they were reconstituted with recovering patients and men on furlough at the Hammerstein training camp. On June 30, 1944, their strength was:

	Officers	NCOs	Men	Total
I./23	9	23	327	369 actual
I./24	6	50	324	380 actual

Since replacements from the *SS* Armored Grenadier Training and Replacement Battalion 11 were sent directly to Estonia because of the Division's high losses, these numbers stayed the same for weeks. To be able to send the battalions back into action, about 1000 members of the *SS* Armored Grenadier Training and Replacement Battalion 11 in Graz were transferred to Hammerstein early in September 1944. After a trip via Vienna, Pressburg, Brno, Breslau, and Posen, the soldiers reached their destination. The next day, 500 men were assigned to each battalion, which were now fully manned. In the I./*SS* Armored Grenadier Regiment 23 "Norge" (*SS Hauptsturmführer* Vogt) there were then only some 40 Norwegians, and in the I./*SS* Armored Grenadier Regiment 24 "Danmark" (*SS Hauptsturmführer* Masche) about 100 Danish volunteers.

On November 16, 1944, the two battalions were ordered subordinated to the 5th *SS* Armored Division "Wiking." Via Bromberg and Thorn, they reached the Modlin depot the next day. From there they marched to the Olcheva area on November 18, 1944, released units of the 542nd Infantry Division, and replaced the III./*SS* Armored Grenadier Battalion 10 "Westland"—consisting mainly of Ukrainian volunteers—which had been shattered in the combat around Nieporent a few days before.[99]

In December 1944 the two battalions moved back to Modlin. At the same time, the order came to the 5th *SS* Armored Division "Wiking" to go to Hungary with the 3rd *SS* Armored Division "Totenkopf" to relieve Budapest. The two battalions of the 11th *SS* Volunteer Armored Grenadier Division "Nordland" remained with the 5th *SS* Armored Division "Wiking" and were loaded onto trains in Modlin on December 31, 1944. On January 1, 1945, the trains reached Komorn. With the 5th *SS* Armored Division "Wiking," readiness

99. The surviving Ukrainians, after various disputes, returned to the 14th Weapon Grenadier Division of the *SS* (Galician No. 1). Compare Rolf Michaelis, *Ukrainians in the Waffen-SS*, Berlin 2000.

areas were immediately set up in the area west of Tata for an attack southward to Budapest. About 6:00 PM the I./*SS* Armored Grenadier Regiment 23 "Norge" was ordered into action to cover the south flank of the attack area. Via Boldogasszony the soldiers advanced to Tata. A few kilometers farther to the southeast there was combat near Felsögalla on 2 and 3 January, and from January 4-12, 1945, in the Bicske area, along with parts of *SS* Armored Regiment 5. The I./*SS* Armored Grenadier Regiment 23 "Norge" was surrounded by Soviet troops at the Hegeyks estate in this fighting and broke out to the west on January 12, 1945. The soldiers gathered in Tarjan and marched on the same day to the Veszprem rest area. The German command halted the attack and regrouped to the south.

On January 16, 1945, the battalion moved to Berhida-Papkeszi. Two days later, the new attempt of the IV. *SS* Armored Corps (*SS Obergruppenführer* and General of the *Waffen-SS* Gille) to free Budapest—now from the west—began. There was heavy fighting in the two battalions' area near Seregelyes and Dinnyes. The battalions were subordinated to the armored battle group of 1st Armored Division (Army) and attacked Pettend along with Armored Grenadier Regiment 1 on January 25, 1945.

On the next day the Red Army began a counterattack, advanced via Acsa on the flank of the IV. *SS* Armored Corps, and met the German units frontally in the Pettend area. Heavy fighting ensued, in which the German troops were able to shoot down some 200 Soviet tanks in a few days—the members of the *SS* Armored Grenadier Battalions "Norge" and "Danmark" shot down 54 of them. The enemy's pressure, though, was so strong that the attempt to relieve Budapest was halted, and the troops had to return to their starting positions in the "Margarethe Position" south of Velencze Lake between Seregelyes and Dinnyes.

The *SS* Command planned to withdraw the two battalions from the 5th *SS* Armored Division "Wiking" and return them to the 11th *SS* Volunteer Armored Grenadier Division "Nordland." But the OKH, at the request of Army Group "Balck," refused to allow a decrease in the fighting power of the subordinated troops. So the company-strong battalions remained in their positions until they were shot down by Soviet tanks and artillery. After that they were taken from the front on February 19, 1945, and refreshed in Urkut, west of Veszprem. The 1./*SS* Armored Grenadier Regiment 23 still had a strength of two officers, two *Unterscharführer*, and 32 men on that day. Despite the transfer of Navy and *Luftwaffe* members, the I./ *SS* Armored Grenadier Regiment 23 "Norge" reached only 40% of full strength by the end of February 1945. On March 1, 1945, *SS Sturmbannführer* Vogt turned the three-company battalion over to *SS Sturmbannführer* Barth and took over *SS* Armored Reconnaissance Battalion 5 in Karpolsk.

The Combat of the I. Battalions of *SS* Armored Grenadier Regiments 23 and 24
(January 2-March 22, 1945)

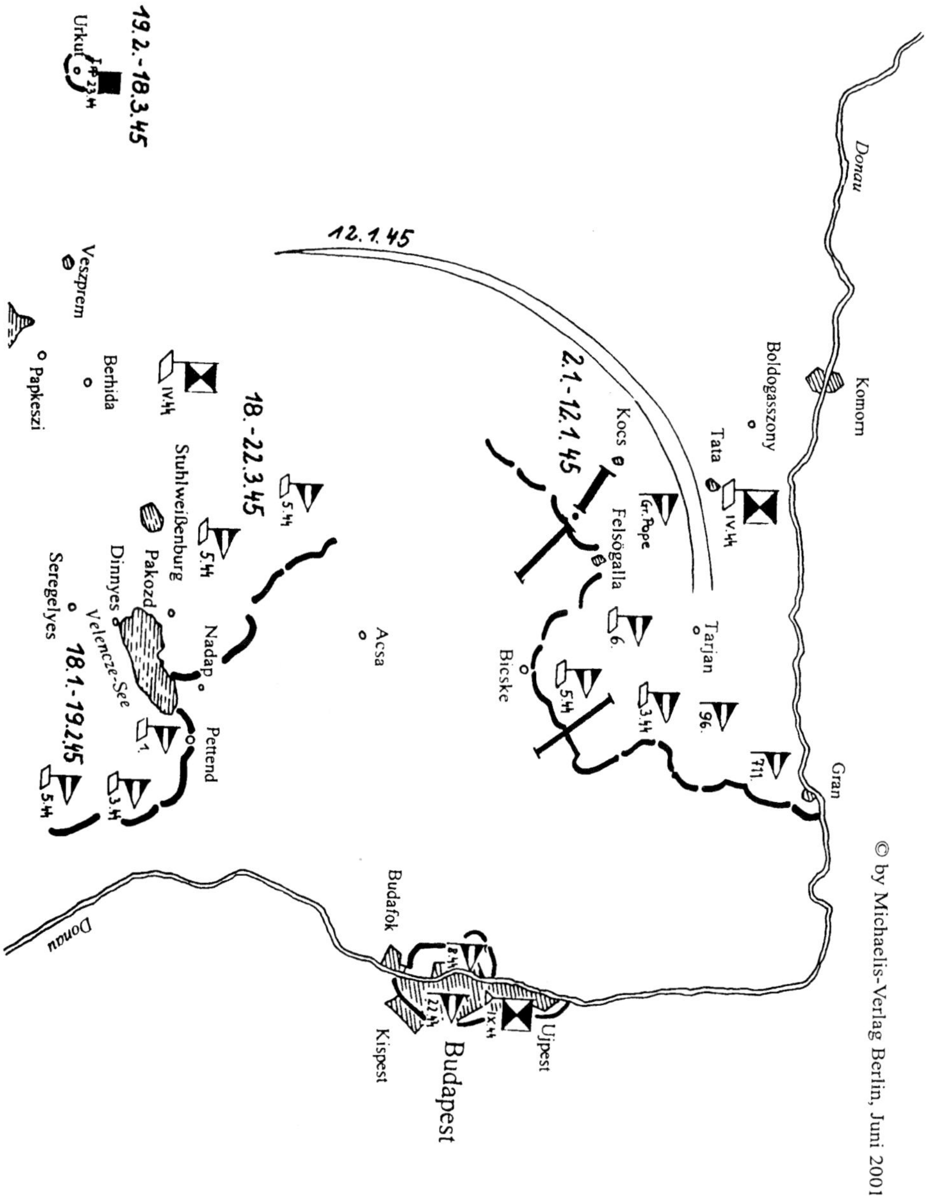

On March 6, 1945, the unsuccessful German offensive of the newly transferred 6th (*SS*) Armored Army with the I. and II. *SS* Armored Corps in the direction of Budapest began. The I./*SS* Armored Grenadier Regiment 24 "Danmark" was subordinated to the battle group of the 3rd *SS* Armored Division "Totenkopf," which consisted of:

- what remained of the 3rd *SS* Armored Division "Totenkopf," with
- Battle Group of the 232nd (Training) Armored Division,
- Battle Group of the 2nd Hungarian Armored Division,
- 1st Battalion of the 20th Hungarian Infantry Division,
- I./*SS* Armored Grenadier Regiment "Danmark,"
- III./*SS* Regiment "Ney"[100]

On March 14, 1945, it was already clear to Army Group "South" that the Red Army was preparing for a counterattack. When the enemy then began to attack at noon on March 16, 1945, after an hour of drumfire, the German efforts to retake the Hungarian capital were finally halted. In the process of the fast advance by the Soviet troops, the I./*SS* Armored Grenadier Regiment 23 "Norge" was alarmed while it was being reconstituted on March 18, 1945, and advanced via Stuhlweissenburg into the Pakozd area. The *Wehrmacht* report stated on that day:

"*The continued breakthrough attacks of the Bolshevists between Velencze Lake and the Felsögalla area came to a stop in our defensive fire north of Stuhlweissenburg or were caught by advanced forces in the hilly land north of Mor.*"

The next day the Battalion took positions southwest of Nadap. The OKW reported on that day:

"*Between Stuhlweissenburg and Felsögalla, the enemy continued his attacks with some 20 rifle divisions and numerous armored troops, and was able to increase the breakthrough area along the ends of the Veltes Mountains to the northeast.*"

100. The *SS* Battle Group "Ney" was created in October 1944, and functioned with its original 300 men as a securing company for *SS* Volunteer Artillery Regiment 22. On December 25, 1944, the unit, already at battalion strength at that time, was taken from the 22nd *SS* Volunteer Cavalry Division and subordinated to the IV. *SS* Armored Corps. As of January 1, 1945, the *SS* Battle Group, meanwhile grown to two battalions, took part in the first attempt to relieve Budapest, the I. Battalion with the 3rd *SS* Armored Division "Totenkopf," and the II. Battalion with the 5th *SS* Armored Division "Wiking." On January 11, 1945, the III. Battalion reported its readiness for action. The total strength of the *SS* Battle Group "Ney" thus numbered some 2000 men. On April 1, 1945, the staff of the battle group, now called the *SS* Regiment "Ney," transferred to Birkfeld in Styria. Meanwhile, divided into four battalions, the I. Battalion was assigned to the *SS* Battle Group "Schweitzer," the II. Battalion to the 1st People's Mountain Division, and the IV. (Replacement) Battalion to the Arko 3—all in the III. Armored Corps (Army) within the 6th Army. The III. Battalion (710 men) remained with the Battle Group of the 3rd *SS* Armored Division "Totenkopf" in the I. *SS* Armored Corps (6th Armored Army).

When the surrounding of the 5th *SS* Armored Division "Wiking" in Stuhlweissenburg became a threat on March 21, 1945, the Division Leader, *SS Oberführer* Ullrich, ordered, contrary to Hitler's order, that the city be given up. The hard-hitting units broke through to the southwest and connected with the 9th *SS* Armored Division "Hohenstaufen" in the Berhida-Papkeszi area.

Very decimated again—among others, *SS Sturmbannführer* Barth had fallen—the rest of the *SS* "Norge" Battalion marched with the scattered units of the 5th *SS* Armored Division "Wiking" to the gathering area of the division in Fürstenfeld at the end of March 1945. From there the units went into the so-called Reich Guard positions early in April. For the remainder of the I./*SS* Armored Grenadier Regiment 23 under the command of *SS Obersturmführer* Radke, this meant the Gleisdorf area north of Feldbach. After the Red Army had moved their focal point northward toward Vienna, all became quiet in the positions north of Feldbach. The soldiers moved via Graz, Bruck, Murau, Tamsweg, and Mauterndorf along with the 5th *SS* Armored Division "Wiking" to Radstadt on May 8, 1945, reaching it on May 12, 1945. Here they were taken prisoner by the Americans. A former member recalls:

"*As ROB in the staff of I./*SS *Armored Grenadier Regiment 23 'Norge' I led a radio troop. The Commander was* SS Hauptsturmführer *Fritz Vogt. He bore the Knight's Cross and received the Oak Leaves in March 1945 for his action at Pettend Castle, Hungary. There Vogt with his armored grenadiers and a battalion of King Tigers had wiped out a Soviet tank brigade. But I got back to the troops only on February 11, 1945, after being in the hospital. In December 1944 I had been hit in both feet with several small splinters from a grenade launcher shell. The medic had presumably not worked cleanly in removing them, or because he could not get my boots off, the small scars were very infected, and in the first week of January, after an advance toward Budapest, I had to leave the troops. At St. Pölten I was able to heal, and then off I went back to Hungary. Before our regiment's battles in Pomerania we had only heard things on the edge; there was no direct link. There were Norwegians all over the place, only as showpieces—in our 1st Battalion there were, besides Germans and Austrians, comrades from Romania and Yugoslavia—plus groups of* Luftwaffe *and Navy men. In March 1945* SS Sturmbannführer *Vogt took command of Armored Reconnaissance Battalion 5, and since I was wounded in the same month near Varpalota, Hungary, I did not get to know the next commander of the I./*SS *Armored Grenadier Battalion 'Norge.' I went via Baden, near Vienna, to the hospital in Linz. Here I could avoid captivity, but the Americans were quartered in our house until 1950, and I lost all my furniture, stamps, and books.*"

The I./*SS* Armored Grenadier Regiment 24 "Danmark" was still with the Battle Group of the 3rd *SS* Armored Division "Totenkopf" early in April 1945, and marched into American imprisonment in May 1945 after the last battles around Vienna.

The *SS* Battle Group "Schweitzer"

After about 1000 members of the *SS* Armored Grenadier Training and Replacement Battalion 11 from Graz had been sent to Pomerania early in September 1944 to refill the two first battalions of *SS* Armored Grenadier Regiments 23 and 24, the battalion refilled itself in the next few weeks from recovered men and newly inducted recruits. In the spring of 1945 it again had a strength of around 1000 men.

When the Red Army reached the Reich Protection position before Steinamanger at the end of March 1945, the *SS* Armored Grenadier Training and Replacement Battalion 11 was alarmed in Graz-Wetzelsdorf on March 30, 1945, and ordered into the threatened area. The next day the six rifle companies under the command of *SS Sturmbannführer* Schweitzer reached the area south of Rechnitz in Burgenland on mail buses and was subordinated to the "Krause" Division Group of the III. Armored Corps. The Corps thus commanded:

- the 1st Folk Mountain Division (Lieutenant General Wittmann),
- the Division Group "Krause" (Lieutenant General Krause),[101]
- the Arko 3 (colonel Semmer),
- the "Motschmann" Blocking Group (*SS* Police Regiment 13).

The "Krause" Division Group was to occupy the space between the 1st Folk Mountain Division as its right neighbor and, to the left, the army border, and consisted of:

- the Field Training Battalion of the 3rd Armored Division,
- two company-strength battle groups of Folk Launcher Brigade 17,
- one flak regiment,
- the *SS* Armored Grenadier Training and Replace Battalion 11,
- parts of the Hungarian *SS* Regiment "Ney,"
- a Mountain *Jäger* Training Battalion,
- a Mountain Veterinary Replacement Company,
- a Cavalry Replacement Squadron.

After troops of the Soviet 6th Guard Armored Corps had occupied Rechnitz[102] without a fight on the morning of March 30, 1945, Lieutenant General Krause ordered the *SS* Armored Grenadier Training and Replacement Battalion 11, now known as the *SS* Battle Group "Schweitzer," to win back the town. Despite a lack of support from heavy weapons, the mostly young recruits of 16 years old and up were able to occupy Rechnitz about 1100

101. See Appendix 9.
102. Early in the 1990s a television team went to Rechnitz to check a rumor that at the end of March 1945 about 180 Hungarian Jews, who were being used to build fortifications, were said to have been shot. Despite several years of research and searches with technical devices, no human remains could be found.

AM on 1 April. Two days later the Battle Group tried to connect with the Mountain *Jäger* Replacement Battalion fighting around Schachendorf. On the afternoon of 4 April, the Red Army was able to enclose the "Schweitzer" Battle Group and cause high losses from steady artillery fire. In this situation, *SS Sturmbannführer* Schweitzer decided to break out.

On the night of April 6, 1945, the breakthrough in the direction of Oberwart began. The next day there was wild woodland fighting with two Soviet regiments. On the morning of April 8, 1945, the young soldiers reached the German main battle line again and gathered near Grafendorf. By 10 April, about 150 survivors of the formerly 1200-man *SS* Battle Group met there. *SS Sturmbannführer* Schweitzer, decorated with the Knight's Cross on 14 April for the recapture of Rechnitz, was wounded during the breakthrough and turned the survivors over to *Untersturmführer* Roller.

Roller led the company-strength Battle Group southward into the area around Hartberg, where the soldiers were subordinated to Arko 3. The last fighting took place near Grafendorf and Rohrbach from 15 to 18 April. Early in May 1945 the company crossed the Enns into American imprisonment. The *SS* Battle Group "Schweitzer," which Lieutenant General Krause described as "*a very good troop*," had lost some 600 dead and wounded, plus almost 300 missing, a large number of whom must be regarded as dead, in the senseless order to retake Rechnitz and the resulting situation (fighting back to the German lines).

The Action of the *SS* Battle Group "Schweitzer" in the Reich Protection position, April 1-May 8, 1945

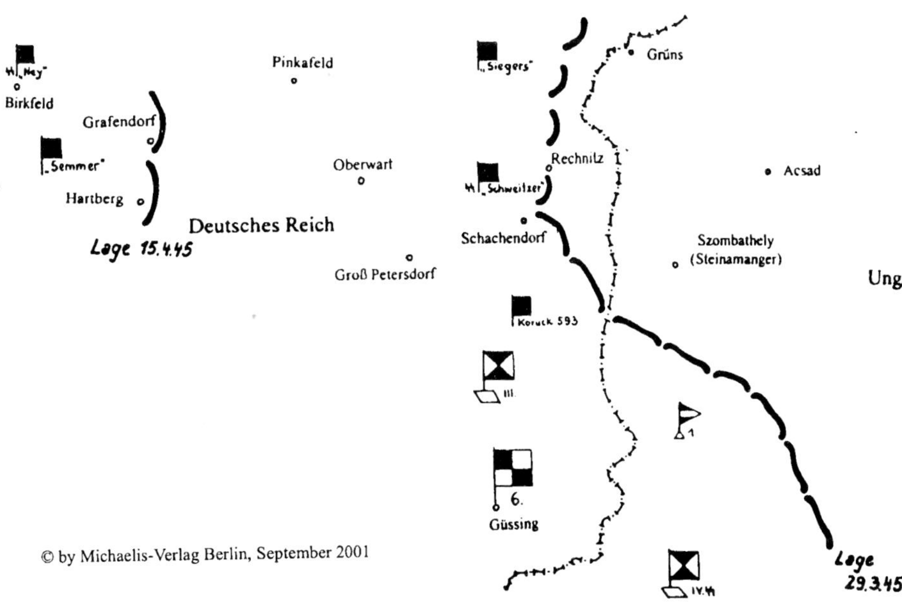

Afterword

The 11th *SS* Volunteer Armored Grenadier Division "Nordland" belongs among the noteworthy units that saw service on the German side during World War II. The formation of the Division in 1943 not only caused problems in equipping and training, but also the difficulty of creating a homogeneous troop. Himmler's plans to build the unit into a Germanic *SS* Corps of Northern European volunteer soldiers came to grief not only from the already hopeless situation of the German Reich, but also from the lack of interest of the Danes, Norwegians, and—neutral—Swedes to be placed in such a framework. After disagreements with the political leaders of the occupied Scandinavian countries, about 12,000 ethnic Germans from Romania had to be integrated into the unit during the course of its service. Thus, they formed the majority of the Division's members.

Under the command of *SS Gruppenführer* and Lieutenant General of the *Waffen-SS* von Scholz, the officer and NCO corps were yet able to form an above-average troop, which was at the heart of the action almost daily since January 1944. They suffered heavy losses in covering the German withdrawal from Russia in the area of the Oranienbaum Pocket to Estonia and the heavy fighting on the Narva front, the Tannenberg position, and at Dorpat. There followed the hasty action before Riga, and the preparation to force the breakout of the German troops from Courland to East Prussia. Known as a strong fighting formation, the Division was withdrawn from Courland and was briefly able to liberate the enclosed city of Arnswalde in the 1945 Pomeranian offensive. Since Hitler wanted to have the Stettin-Altdamm bridgehead as the starting point for a new offensive toward Danzig, the 11th *SS* Volunteer Armored Grenadier Division "Nordland" was decimated in carrying out this order. With only 30% of its full strength, the Division went into the final fighting around the German capital and was shattered there.

Appendices

Appendix I
Chronology

3/3/1943-9/1943 Formation of the Division in Germany
9/1943-12/1943 Transfer to Croatia, further training
12/1943-2/2/1944 Action in Russia (Oranienbaum Pocket and withdrawal to the Narva)
1/26/1944-1/30/1944 Action of *SS* Armored Reconnaissance Battalion 11 in Battle Group "Wengler"
2/2/1944-9/21/1944 Fighting in Estonia
7/13/1944-9/17/1944 *SS* Battle Group "Saalbach" (*SS* Armored Reconnaissance Battalion 11) at Jakobstadt and Dorpat
9/14/1944-10/28/1944 *SS* Battalion z.b.V. "Nordland" in 4th *SS* Volunteer Armored Grenadier Brigade "Nederland"
9/22/1944-1/30/1945 Participation in Courland battles in Latvia
2/5/1945-2/20/1945 Action in Pomerania: Arnswalde, Stargard, Altdamm
2/21/1945-3/18/1945 Refreshing and Army Group reserve between Gartz and Schwedt
3/18/1945-5/2/1945 Division's final action around and in Berlin
11/16/1944-5/8/1945 Action of both battalions of *SS* Armored Grenadier Regiments 23 and 24 in 5th *SS* Armored Division "Wiking" in Hungary and Ostmark
3/30/1945-5/8/1945 Action of Battle Group "Schweitzer" (*SS* Armored Grenadier Training and Replacement Battalion 11) in Reich Protection position

Appendix 2

Himmler's Memo on the Western and Northern European Volunteers in the *Waffen-SS* in 1943

"*The Germanic Corps shall consist of two divisions: the 'Wiking' Division and the new 'Nordland' Division to be formed. The 'Wiking' Division is a pure* SS *division, whose men without exception correspond to the requirements of the* SS *and are members of the* SS. *The 'Nordland' Division is an* SS *volunteer division whose men only partially correspond to the requirements of the* SS *and are members of the* SS, *while the large majority of them correspond to the requirements for acceptance in the k. v. Army or g.v.F.*

I. In the refreshing of the 'Wiking' Division, the following is to be considered.

The 'Wiking' Division presumably has at present a lack of 5000 men. In addition, out of the present complement of the 'Wiking' Division comes half the complement of the 'Nordland' Standard, all of them Norwegian,[103] *who are in it, and a portion of the German* SS *men. When I add today a contingent of around 2000 men from the 'Nordland' Standard, the lack in the 'Wiking' Division is about 1000 men.*

In the 'Wiking' Division, out of the remaining part of the Nordland Standard, consisting of Germans and Finns, a German-Finnish Regiment becomes formed, for which I suggest the name 'Kalevala.' The question of replacement of the Finns serving us today, whose service time runs out in May, must first be made definite through negotiations with Finland, the conducting of which by us I suggest with the approval of the Foreign Office.[104]

For the 'Germania' Standard of the 'Wiking' Division I declare anew that this regiment shall include members of all peoples who have provided volunteers to the SS. *Thus Danes,*[105] *Germans, Estonians, Finns, Liechtensteiners, Flemings, Netherlanders, Swedes, and Swiss.*

103. On June 22, 1941, the *SS* Standard "Nordland" served with, among others, 294 Norwegians and 216 Danes, and 834 Finns finally formed the III. Battalion. The numbers of Norwegians and Danes did not change much—numerous Scandinavian volunteers, on the other hand, joined the Legions. The replacements for the *SS* Standard principally about equaled the occurring—sometimes heavy losses. An overview of the Germanic volunteers in the *Waffen-SS* as of January 15, 1942, shows the following picture:

1218 Norwegians served in the "Norwegen" Legion and only 665 in the *SS* Standard "Nordland"—1,164 Danes (including the so-called North Schleswig ethnic Germans) were in the "Danmark" Free Corps and 1,235 in the *SS* Standard "Nordland."

104. The Finnish government opposed the further duty of the *SS* volunteers—effective July 11, 1943, the Finnish Battalion was disbanded. From then on, the men served in the Finnish Army.

105. According to these plans, the Danes of the *SS* Standard "Nordland" should be transferred to the *SS* Standard "Germania."

The sun-wheel of Wiking, that to date was the symbol of the Division on their vehicles and that has gained a famous admiration, is to be turned over by the Wiking Division as the symbol for the mirror of the new Division 'Nordland' as a godfatherly gift. For the 'Wiking' Division I imagine a new symbol of the dragon-head of a Viking ship.

II. Establishment of the "Nordland" Division

The 'Nordland' Division is structured exactly like the 'Wiking' Division. It is thus composed of two armored grenadier regiments, one light regiment, in which a reconnaissance battalion and a Volkswagen battalion are included, armored regiment, artillery regiment, and all other troop units. The composition and formation of the individual regiments is to take place under the following principles.

1. Armored Grenadier Regiment 'Danmark': The 'Danmark' Free Corps forms the cadre of the regiment; it presently has a strength of some 650 men. The replacement company, which is located in Mogilev at this time, will also be sent on the march to the regiment. The vacancies are to be filled by Danes who are being recruited in Denmark at this time, as well as by Danes who are in Sennheim, as long as they are not sent on the march to the 'Wiking' Division, and by Germans. To this Danish regiment, SS Obersturmbannführer *Martinsen, as well as Dane Neergard Jacobsen, recently promoted by me to* SS Sturmbannführer, *come into question as Battalion Commanders. As Company Chiefs, three Danes are presently available:* SS Hauptsturmführer *Sorensen and* SS Obersturmführer *Paulsen, and Worsoe Larsen.* SS Hauptsturmführer *Kai Hansen can be used in the staff. The extraction of the 'Danmark' Free Corps from the I.* SS *Brigade in the very near future is a prerequisite for this establishment. The First Battalion of the 'Danmark' Regiment is justified, in case importance is given to it by the Danes themselves, to bear 'Freikorps Danmark' on their sleeves as well.*

2. Armored Grenadier Regiment 'Nederland': The staff and the bulk of the Regiment are formed of the 'Niederlande' Legion. For it, a strength of around 1700 men is to be presumed. It is to be completed with further volunteers from Sennheim, the replacement units, and the Netherlanders, as well as Germans. Here too, in this regiment, it is to be striven for that at least two battalion commanders be Netherlanders, plus a number of the company chiefs. The service of Flemings in the 'Nederland' Regiment is strictly forbidden.

3. The Light or Advance Regiment 'Norge': Its cadre is formed by the 'Norwegen' Legion, which along with a replacement company and after calculating the men who will presumably go to their homeland because of their expired and not renewed contract, will include some 600 men. It is to be assumed that a number of volunteers in service—about 150 to 200—will come back. The vacancies of this regiment, including only two companies, are to be filled with Norwegian volunteers, from the replacement units, and from Sennheim, as well as from Norway itself. Two Norwegians are available as battalion commanders: SS Sturmbannführer *Quist,*[106] *whose use I consider politically necessary despite all considerations, and* SS Hauptsturmführer *Vinson, who presently commands the Legion as a deputy.* SS Sturmbannführer Lie,[107] *as long as he can stay in service, is to be used best as an* SS Sturmbannführer *in the staff of the regiment or in the division. As company chiefs, three company leaders from the 'Norwegen' Legion, plus Company Leaders Lindwig and Swen, who are coming back from Norway as recovered, are available. As a regiment adjutant, it is best to use* SS Hauptsturmführer *Raddatz. As another* Hauptsturmführer *in the staff, the present* SS Obersturmführer *Koerner, who would be promoted to* SS Hauptsturmführer *and knows the Norwegians and the Norwegian Legion thoroughly. In the other units of the Division, artillery, armored, and other technical troops, 80 to 90% Germans are to be used. The men for the German part of the Division are to be taken from native Germans and ethnic Germans, who can be taken as much as possible from the German ethnic group in Romania.*

III. As the Commander of the Division I appoint SS Brigadeführer *von Scholz.*[108]

IV. The refreshing of the 'Wiking' Division is best prepared for now at the Field Recruit Depot of the 'Wiking' Division in Uspenskaya, by sending recruits with 4 or 8 weeks of training there as quickly as possible.

V. The non-commissioned officers for the new division are to be taken for the most part from veterans of the 'Wiking' Division, the Legion, and the Free Corps. Likewise, German non-commissioned officers can be taken from one of two regiments of the 1st SS *Brigade. In addition, I recommend that of the 1400 non-commissioned officers coming from the Work Service, who have also had one or two years' of* Unterführer *service, also in the field, a portion of 600 to 700 be taken, who after 4 to 6 weeks of training with the weapon and a four-week* Unterführer *course, can be out to use as definitely very good* Unterführer, *who have in particular a very good view of the world. The* Führer *Corps must be established and filled from Germanic corps by exchanging from the 'Wiking' Division by transfer into the ranks of German Junkers of the last year, and by taking in the portion of 30 Norwegian officers, some of whom are in the course at Tölz.*

106. *SS Sturmbannführer* Artur Quist was Commander of the Volunteer Legion "Norwegen" and was decorated with the Iron Cross 2nd and 1st classes.

107. See Appendix 9.

108. See Appendix 9.

VI. From the Estonian Legion are to be taken to fill the 'Germania' Standard and for other units of the division, the 800 racially best, who are fluent in the German language. The about 400 remaining men, along with the replacements still to be expected from Estonia, are to be combined in a horse-drawn grenadier regiment.

This regiment replaces one of the two (mot.) regiments in the 1. SS *Brigade. From this (mot.) regiment, men, non-commissioned officers, and officers can be taken to complete and establish the* SS *Division 'Nordland,' as well as to provide a staff of still lacking officers and non-commissioned officers for the Estonian Grenadier Regiment, completing the remaining regiment.*

The symbol of the 'Nordland' Division is the symbol of the sun-wheel taken from the 'Wiking' Division. This symbol will be worn by all members of the Division on their collar tabs. All members of the SS*, like the* SS *men of the 'Prinz Eugen' Division, the* SS *Brigade, and the Police, wear the embroidered runes on the left side of their chest.*

VII. From the 'Flandern' Legion, with the addition of German officers and a very small number of German non-commissioned officers, a grenadier regiment is to be formed. The proved 'Flandern' Legion will form the cadre of the assault brigade, with a current strength of about 700 men, from additional Flemings from the Replacement Battalion, the Legion, from Sennheim, and from the Flemings to be expected from the continuing recruiting.

With the Flemish men it is to be made sure that they are used primarily as replacements for the 'Langemarck' Regiment. As for the rest, as replacements for the 'Germania' Standard or replacements in the technical armored, artillery, etc. troops of the 'Reich,' 'Totenkopf,' 'Wiking,' and Police Divisions. The Flemish Grenadier Regiment will be subordinated to the Police Division.

VIII. I request that it always be kept in mind that in the apportioning of the replacements the error of assigning Germanic volunteers to inappropriate troop units of the Waffen-SS *be strictly avoided. I request that an order from me be presented to all units of the* Waffen-SS *by which this be maintained, Germanic volunteers who do not belong to their troop unit be reported and sent back at once. Thus,* SS Obergruppenführer *Rediess*[109] *has reported that in the various E-units and units of the* Waffen-SS *about 180 Norwegian volunteers are scattered. The 'Wiking' and 'Nordland' Divisions, composed of mixed German and other Germanic volunteers, are to make sure that in all the troop units in which the Germanic volunteers are not present in the majority, they not be used as bakers, butchers, or in the columns. Unless it may be that their level of ability does not allow a different use.*

109. See Appendix 9.

IX. The formation of a brigade out of the Walloon Free Corps and French volunteers still requires clarification and political consideration. The order to assemble French volunteers is hereby given. As for the Walloon Legion, I am gradually coming more to the opinion that they be given at first to the Germanic Corps as a Corps Motorcycle Rifle Battalion or something similar as corps troops. The Walloon Legion includes approximately 1,500 men. The 200 to 300 racially best SS men can be added to the 'Wiking' Division or the 'Germania' Standard Tank-Destroyer Battalion and Engineer Battalion."

Appendix 3

Himmler's Memo of July 23, 1943, about the Disagreements with Foreign Party Leaders

"*1. In the middle of the year* [this must mean the beginning of the year; author's note] *I suggested to the* Führer *the establishment of a Germanic* SS *Volunteer Armored Grenadier Division. The* Führer *decided that it should receive the name 'Nordland.' Thereupon the Leader of the NSB in the Netherlands, Mr. Mussert, raised his voice and objected to Netherlanders being included in a 'Nordland' Division. He then gave to understand that the Netherlanders as volunteers could provide the men for a whole division. Thereupon I asked the* Führer *for the establishment order for the* SS *Armored Grenadier Division 'Nederland' that the* Führer *also approved, giving Leader Mussert the opportunity to make his promise come true.*

2. It turned out that both the SS *Armored Grenadier Volunteer Division 'Nordland' and the* SS *Armored Grenadier Volunteer Division 'Nederland' could consist of no more than one-third of the Germanic forces.*

3. It is also clear that vehicles and weapons for two armored grenadier divisions will be obtained with great difficulty and only too late.

4. For this reason I decided, instead of the 2nd Armored grenadier Division 'Nederland,' to set up two horse-drawn brigades. One SS *Volunteer Mountain Brigade 'Norge' that is to be established not in Germany, but in Finland through the* SS *Mountain Division, and one* SS *Volunteer Grenadier Brigade 'Nederland,' which is to be established by the Germanic Corps in Germany at Grafenwöhr.*

5. The SS *Armored grenadier Volunteer Division 'Nordland' shall then consist of Danish, German, Swedish, and Swiss volunteers. The* SS *Mountain Division 'Nord,' in a change of my recently given order, is to give up its Swiss volunteers to the 'Nordland' Division.*

6. The SS *Volunteer Mountain Brigade 'Norge' to be established in Finland surely has more enthusiasm on the front in Karelia than in Russia. This mountain brigade can best represent the Norwegian character within the Germanic total army, namely as mountain troops.*

7. The advantage of the formation of the SS *Volunteer Grenadier Brigade 'Nederland' is as follows:*

It can surely be expected that we will receive a further approximately 3,000 men to add to the presently present 2,500 volunteers. Added to this, a cadre and specialist personnel of 2,000 to 3,000 Germans, so that here we can count a total number of 8,000 men. Thus, we spare ourselves the filling of the already planned Armored Grenadier Division of 5,000 to 6,000 Netherlanders to the total number of 18,000 to 19,000 with Germans, and thus an addition of 13,000 to 14,000 men. I foresee the structure of the brigade as follows: two grenadier regiments of two battalions each and the corresponding regimental units, one artillery regiment of two light battalions and one heavy battalion, tank-destroyer battalions, etc. to two companies. In some cases they will get by with a single company. With this grenadier brigade, a solid basis would be formed for any expansion to a grenadier division, which can be come up with at the moment, in which enough volunteers come from the Netherlands. In addition, this solution has the advantage that we also, in the sense of for future organizational complete concept for a Germanic Wehrmacht, *which consists of Army, Navy, and* Luftwaffe *armored service of the* Waffen-SS *are to be* Reich *institutions, while country contingents shall best represent normal mountain or grenadier divisions.*

I am of the opinion that this grenadier brigade must be made mobile for the Russian terrain in summer and winter by utilizing all experience, and shall be and remain a part of the Germanic Corps. I believe that an armored corps that normally would consist of only two divisions without this, could be utilized very well for flank protection or taking over captured positions, can use a grenadier brigade and later a grenadier division directly subordinated to it.

8. This organizational change would have to be presented and related to the Netherlanders and Norwegians in a rational and respectable form. I am convinced that both will understand these changes and probably even welcome them. The Norwegians, since their troop will then fight in a psychologically tangible closeness to the Norwegian homeland, namely at the Karelian front, and ski and mountain formations are very familiar to the Norwegians; the Netherlanders, because they will then not have the shaming and depressing feeling that a division bears the name 'Nederland' but is made up to a great extent of non-Netherlanders, namely of Germans.

9. As commanders of the two brigades, I think that for the 'Norge' Mountain Brigade I must have a suggestion made; for the 'Nederland' Grenadier Brigade I think, now as before, of SS Oberführer *Wagner,*[110] *who is foreseen for the 'Nederland' Division.*

Appendix 4

Bearers of the Knight's Cross to the Iron Cross

The numbers of Knight's Crosses awarded to the Iron Cross indicate externally the fighting power and utility of a unit. From their first front service in January 1944 on, 29 members of the 11th *SS* Volunteer Armored Grenadier Division "Nordland" received this high recognition to the end of the war. The comparison to the 12th *SS* Armored Division "Das Reich" (including the previous *SS* Reserve Division), which from the western campaign to the end of the war received 73 Knight's Crosses, the absolutely highest number of decorations in the *Waffen-SS*, is shown in the following statistical figures:

SS Division "Nordland" (17 months service) = 1.71 awards per month,
SS Division "Das Reich" (60 months service) = 1.22 awards per month.

Even when one considers the condition that toward the end of the war considerably more Knight's Crosses were awarded than in the first years, a noteworthy picture is shown. The 11th *SS* Volunteer Armored Grenadier Division "Nordland" surely ranked among the best units of the German troops. It is interesting in this respect that within this *SS* unit no "Germanic" volunteer—neither from Denmark, Norway, nor Sweden—was awarded the Knight's Cross to the Iron Cross! In the *SS* Armored Grenadier Regiment 23 "Norge," 12 men, in the *SS* Armored Grenadier Regiment 24 "Danmark," on the other hand, only four members earned the Knight's Cross:

SS Hauptsturmführer Josef Bachmeier (Fhr. II./*SS* Pz.Gren.Rgt. 23)	08/23/44
SS Sturmbannführer Fritz Bunse (Cdr. *SS* Engineer Battalion 11)	01/30/44
SS Unterscharführer Egon Christopherson (7./*SS* Pz.Gren.Rgt. 24)	07/11/44
SS Sturmbannführer Alfred Fischer (Cdr. II./*SS* Pz.Artil.Rgt. 11)	05/09/45
SS Hauptsturmführer Martin Guerz (Fhr. III./*SS* Pz.Gren.Rgt. 23)	08/23/44
SS Hauptsturmführer Heinz Haemel (Fhr. II./*SS* Pz.Gren.Rgt. 24)	06/16/44
SS Oberscharführer Albert Hektor (7./*SS* Pz.Gren.Rgt. 24)	08/23/44

110. See Appendix 9.

SS Hauptsturmführer Ludwig Hoffmann (Fhr. III./*SS* Pz.Gren.Rgt. 23)	05/09/45
SS Obersturmführer Willi und (7./*SS* Pz.Gren.Rgt. 23)	04/20/45
SS Obersturmbannführer Friedrich-Wm. Karl (Cdr. *SS* Pz.Art.Rgt.11)	12/26/44
SS Obersturmbannführer Paul-Albert Kausch (Cdr. *SS* Pz.Abt. 11)	08/23/44
(as Cdr. *SS* Panzer Regiment 11) Oak Leaves to Knight's Cro*SS*	04/23/45
SS Obersturmbannführer Fritz Knöchlein (Cdr. *SS* Pz.Gren.Rgt. 23)	11/16/44
SS Hauptsturmführer Walter Koerner (Adjutant, *SS* Pz.Gren.Rgt. 23)	05/09/45
SS Untersturmführer Georg Langendorf (Fhr. 5./Pz.Aufkl.Abt. 11)	03/12/44
SS Hauptscharführer Siegfried Luengen (Fhr. 6./*SS* Pz.Gren.Rgt. 23)	11/16/44
SS Sturmbannführer Hermann Potschka (Cdr. II./*SS* Pz.Art,Rgt. 11)	12/26/44
SS Obersturmführer Rudolf Rott (Chief 1./*SS* Panzer *Abetilung* 11)	02/28/45
SS Hauptsturmführer Rudolf Saalbach (Cdr. *SS* Panzer.Aufkl.Abt. 11)	03/12/44
SS Sturmbannführer Karl-H. Schulz-Streeck (Cdr. *SS* Stu.G.Abt. 11)	05/02/45
SS Brigadeführer Fritz von Scholz (as Cdr 11. *SS* Div. "Nordland,"	
Oak leaves to Knight's Cross	03.12.44
(As *SS* Gruppenführer & Div.Cdr.) Swords to Knight's Cross	08/08/44
SS Sturmbannführer Willi Schweitzer (Cdr. *SS* Pz.Gren.Ausb.Btl. 11)	04/14/45
SS Obersturmführer Walter Seebach (Fhr. 5./*SS* Pz.Gren.Rgt. 24)	03/12/44
SS Hauptsturmführer Richard Spoerle (Fhr. II./*SS* Pz.Gren.Rgt. 23)	11/16/44
SS Obersturmbannführer Arnold Stoffers (Cdr. *SS* Pz.Gren.Rgt. 23)	03/12/44
SS Oberscharführer Philipp Wild (1./*SS* Panzer *Abteilung* 11)	03/21/44
SS Hauptsturmführer Fritz Vogt (Cdr. 1./*SS* Pz.Gren.Rgt. 23)	03/16/45
SS Brigadeführer Joachim Ziegler (Cdr. 11. *SS* Div. "Nordland")	09/05/44

Appendix 5
Bearers of the German Cross in Gold

Only one "Germanic" volunteer—Per Sörensen—received the German Cross in Gold! In the *SS* Armored Grenadier Regiment 23 "Norge" five men, in the *SS* Armored Grenadier Regiment 24 "Danmark" three members, and in the *SS* Armored Battalion 11 seven soldiers were awarded this medal for bravery.

SS Obersturmbannführer Helmut von Bockelberg	08/19/44
SS Untersturmführer Richard Braunstein (St.Kp./*SS* Pz. Abt. 11)	10/27/44
SS Obersturmkführer Heinz Fechner (1./*SS* Pz.Gren.Rgt. 23)	03/12/44
SS Obersturmführer Erhard Goettlich (6./*SS* Pz.Gren.Rgt. 23)	04/30/44
SS Hauptsturmführer Artur Grathwol (4./*SS* Pz.Abt. 11)	08/29/44
SS Obersturmführer Rolf Holzboog (*SS* Flak.Abt. 11)	09/17/44

SS Obersturmführer Walter Koerner (8./*SS* Pz.Gren.Rgt. 23) 04/28/44
SS Hauptscharführer Kurt Kuehne (4./*SS* Pz.Abt. 11) 09/17/44
SS Oberscharführer Karl Kutsch (9./*SS* Pz.Gren.Rgt. 23) 01/07/44
SS Obersturmführer Georg Langendorf (5./Pz.Aufkl.Abt. 11) 03/30/45
SS Obersturmbannführer Walter Ploew (ZZ Flak-Abt. 11) 01/13/45
SS Sturmbannführer Hermann Potschka (III./*SS* Pz.Art.Rgt. 11) 03/29/44
SS Untersturmführer Karl von Renteln (*SS* Pz.Jaeg.Abt. 11) 11/28/44
SS Obersturmführer Rudolph Rott (1./*SS* Pz. Abt. 11) 12.18.44
SS Hauptsturmführer Per Sörensen (*SS* Pz.Gren.Rgt. 24) 10/14/44
SS Obersturmführer Ernst-Richard Stuebben (3./*SS* Pz. Abt. 11) 10/27/44
SS Hauptscharführer Karl Theilacker (7./*SS* Pz.Gren.Rgt. 23) 11/28/44
SS Hauptsturmführer Guenther Viercks (7./*SS* Pz.Art.Rgt. 11) 03/25/44
SS Oberscharführer Alfred Wedel (4./*SS* Pz. Abt. 11) 03/30/45
SS O'stubaf. Hermengild Graf von Westphalen (*SS* Pz.Gren.Rgt. 24) 04/23/44
SS Standardtenoberjunker Georg Wille (4./*SS* Pz. Abt. 11) 09.17.44

Appendix 6
Bearers of the German Cross in Silver

SS Sturmbannführer Siegfried Conrad (11. *SS* Pz.Gren.Div.) 01/10/45
SS Sturmbannführer Friedrich Glaesker (*SS* Div. Supply Train 11) 06/02/44
SS Hauptscharführer Kurt Heindel (5./*SS* Pz.Gren.Rgt. 23) 04/29/45
SS Hauptsturmführer d.R. Joachim Tiburtius (11. *SS* Pz.Gren.Div.) 02/21/45

Appendix 7
Bearers of the Close Combat Medal in Gold

SS Obersturmführer Walter Seebach (Fhr. 5./*SS* Pz.Gren.Rgt. 24) 02/16/45
SS Sturmbannführer Rudolf Ternedde (Cdr. *SS* Pz.Gren.Rgt. 24) 04/23/45
SS Oberscharführer Karl Viehmann (14./*SS* Pz.Gren.Rgt. 23) 04/03/45
SS Hauptscharführer Willi Wettstein (*SS* Pz.Gren.Rgt. 23) [no date]

Appendix 8

Field Post Numbers and Commanders

Division Staff	F.P. No. 33 316	*SS Brigadeführer* Fritz von Scholz
		SS Brigadeführer Joachim Ziegler
		SS Brigadeführer Dr. Gustav Krukenberg
1 a		*SS Oberstubaf.* Helmut von Vollard-Bockelberg
		SS Sturmbannführer Ruediger Weitzdürfer
		SS Obersturmbannf. Erich von Bock und Polach
		SS Obersturmbannführer Herbert Wienczek
1 b		*SS Sturmbannführer* Gerhard Noatzke
		SS Hauptsturmführer Joachim Tiburtius
1 c		*SS Obersturmführer* Walter Felts
		SS Hauptsturmführer Günther Greef
II a		*SS Sturmbannführer* Albert Bergfeld
		SS Sturmbannführer Dr, Kurt Witten
		SS Hauptsturmführer Arthur Ruhnow
IV a		*SS Sturmbannführer* Siegfried Conrad
		SS Sturmbannführer Walter Meyer
IV b		*SS Standartenführer* Dr. Hans Schlosser

***SS* Volunteer Armored Grenadier Regiment 23 "Norge"**

Staff	F.P. No. 41 89	*SS Obersturmbannführer* Wolfgang Joerchel
		SS Obersturmbannführer Arnold Stoffers
		SS Obersturmbannführer Fritz Knöchlein
		SS Sturmbannführer Wilhelm Körbel
		SS Sturmbannführer Wilhelm Ternedde
I. Battalion	F.P. No. 32 298	*SS Sturmbannführer* Finn Finson
		SS Sturmbannführer Fritz Vogl
II. Battalion	F.P. No. 42 264	*SS Sturmbannführer* Wilhelm Körbel
		SS Sturmbannführer Siegfried Scheibe
		SS Hauptsturmführer Josef Bachmeier
		SS Hauptsturmführer Richard Spörle
III. Battalion	F.P. No. 32 878	*SS Sturmbannführer* Hans-Heinrich Lohmann
		SS Sturmbannführer Martin Guerz
		SS Hauptsturmführer Ludwig Hoffmann
14. Company	F.P. No. 38 387	
15. Company	F.P. No. 33 725	
16. Company	F.P. No. 43 509	

SS Volunteer Armored Grenadier Regiment 24 "Danmark"

Staff	F.P. No. 35 408	*SS Obersturmbannf.* Hermengild von Westphalen
		SS Obersturmbannführer Albrecht Krügel
		SS Obersturmbannführer Wilhelm Körbel
		SS Obersturmbannführer Rudolf Klotz
		SS Sturmbannführer Per Sierensen
		SS Sturmbannführer Rudolf Ternedde
I. Battalion	F.P. No. 40 670	*SS Obersturmbannführer* Knud-Börge Martinsen
		SS Hauptsturmführer Karl Wichmann
		SS Sturmbannführer Siegfried Scheibe
II. Battalion	F.P. No. 37 826	*SS Hauptsturmführer* Kurt Walther
		SS Hauptsturmführer Heilz Hämel
		SS Sturmbannführer Albert Bergfeld
		SS Hauptsturmführer Hermann Im Masche
		SS Sturmbannführer Per Sörensen
III. Battalion	F.P. No. 34 531	*SS Sturmbannführer* Neergard Jakobsen
		SS Sturmbannführer Hans Kappus
		SS Hauptsturmführer Rudolf ternedde
13. Company	F.P. No. 32 777	
14. Company	F.P. No. 35 637	
15. Company	F.P. No. 41 702	
16. Company	F.P. No. 33 362	

SS Volunteer Armored Artillery Regiment 11

Staff	F.P. No. 42 973	*SS Obersturmbannführer* Friedrich-Wilhelm Karl
I. Battalion	F.P. No. 35 179	*SS Hauptsturmführer* Otto Kroll
II. Battalion	F.P. No. 32 895	*SS Hauptsturmführer* Hermann Fischmann
III. Battalion	F.P. No. 34 885	*SS Hauptsturmführer* Hermann Potschka

SS Armored Regiment (Battalion) II "Hermann von Salza"

Staff	F.P. No. 32 192	*SS Obersturmbannführer* Paul-Albert Kausch
I. Battalion		*SS Hauptsturmführer* Arthur Grathwol
II. Battalion		*SS Sturmbannführer* Otto Paetsch
(s. *SS*-Pz.Abt. 503)		*SS Sturmbannführer* Friedrich Herzig
SS Pz.Aufkl.Abt.11	No. 33 756	*SS Sturmbannführer* Rudolf Saalbach
SS Nachr.Abt. 11	No. 43 843	*SS Sturmbannführer* Rüdiger Weitzdörfer
		SS Obersturmbannführer Eugen Schlotter
		SS Hauptsturmführer Schnick
SS Assault Gun Btl. 11		*SS Hauptsturmführer* Ernst Röntsch
SS Flak Btl. 11	No. 43 111	*SS Obersturmbannführer* Walter Plöw
		SS Sturmbannführer Emil Kurz
SS Field Repl. Btl.11	No.59 858	*SS Obersturmbannführer* Franz Lang

SS Engineer Btl. 11	No. 38 749	*SS Sturmbannführer* Fritz Bunse
		SS Sturmbannführer Hermann Voss
		SS Sturmbannführer Wilhelm Stapper
SS Econ.Btl. 11	No. 39 384	*SS Sturmbannführer* Siegfried Conrad
SS Med. Btl. 11	No. 39 160	

Appendix 9
Biographies

Wilhelm Berlin was born in Cologne on April 28, 1889. He entered military service as a *Fähnrich* on March 12, 1909, and was named a lieutenant on January 27, 1910. After taking part in World War I and serving in the *Reichswehr*, he was promoted to Colonel on April 1, 1936—effective October 12, 1937, Commander of Artillery Regiment 33. As major general (since March 1, 1940) he directed the Artillery School at Jüterbog from October 10, 1940, to April 3, 1943. Promoted to Lieutenant General on March 1, 1942, he was the Deputy Commander of the 58th Infantry Division as of May 1, 1943. On 7 June of that year Berlin took command of the 227th Infantry Division. From May 11 to June 15, 1944, he commanded the XXVI. Army Corps. He was then transferred to the OKH in Berlin as General of the Artillery and, as General of the Artillery (October 1, 1944)—from February 27 to April 18, 1945, commanded the CI. Army Corps. He had been decorated with the Knight's Cross on March 6, 1944.

Walter Graf von Brockdorff-Ahlefeldt was born in Perleberg on July 13, 1887, and entered military service as a *Fahnenjunker* on April 25, 1904. In 1908 he served as a lieutenant in *Jäger* Battalion 3. After World War I he first commanded Infantry Regiment 8, and later the 23rd Division in the *Reichswehr* and *Wehrmacht*. His promotion to Major General on April 1, 1937, was followed by that to Lieutenant General on March 1, 1939. As General of the Infantry (August 1, 1940) he commanded the II. Army Corps and was decorated with the Knight's Cross and Oak Leaves. Seriously ill, Brockdorff-Ahlefeldt died on January 19, 1943.

Theodor Busse was born in Frankfurt on the Oder on December 15, 1897, and entered the Royal Prussian Army as a *Fahnenjunker* on December 1, 1915. On February 1, 1917, he was named lieutenant in Grenadier Regiment 12. His participation in World War I was followed by service in the *Reichswehr*. As of July 1, 1937, Busse was 1st General Staff Officer of the 22nd Division. Named Lieutenant Colonel on February 1, 1939, he served in the Army General Staff when the Polish campaign began. On September 1, 1940, he became the 1st General Staff Officer in the staff of the 11th Army, and after his promotion to Colonel (August 1, 1941) he held the same position in Army Group "Don," later "South." Under his simultaneous promotion to Major General, Busse was Chief of the General

Staff of Army Group "South" as of March 1, 1943. Promoted to Lieutenant General on September 1, 1943, he commanded the 121st Infantry Division as of July 10, 1944. A month later Busse, decorated with the Knight's Cross and General of the Infantry since November 1, 1944, commanded the I. Army Corps and, as of January 9, 1945, the 9th Army.

Frits Clausen was born in Abenra, North Schleswig, in 1893, and served in the German Army in World War I. Later he studied veterinary medicine in Germany and joined the Danish National Socialist Worker Party in Denmark. In 1933 he became its leader. His hopes of taking over the Danish government with German help in 1940 were not fulfilled. Hitler had no interest in the DNSAP, since Clausen had no backing from the people. He fell victim to alcohol, volunteered for the *Waffen-SS*, and was inducted as an *SS Obersturmbannführer* on November 1, 1943. In February 1944 he was transferred to the Nerve Hospital in Würzburg for a cure. In May of that year he withdrew from his office as party leader, was expelled from the DNSAP in November, and died of a heart attack while imprisoned after the war ended.

Alfred Jacobi was born in Bremen on July 29, 1884, and joined the military as a *Fahnenjunker* on September 16, 1902. On January 27, 1905, he was promoted to Lieutenant in Infantry Regiment 60. After World War I Jacobi was released at the rank of Major on December 31, 1919. As of May 17, 1921, he serried in the police, and on October 15, 1935, he joined the Army as a colonel. Until November 26, 1940, Jacobi belonged to Defense Zone Command I in Stettin. Then he commanded Infantry Regiment 570 and, after promotion to Major General (January 1, 1941), Field Command 748 as of July 22, 1941. On January 18, 1942, he took over the Gomel Command and was given command of the 201st Securing Division on May 20, 1942. Decorated with the German Cross in Gold, the Lieutenant General (March 1, 1943) retired from service on February 28, 1945.

Paul-Albert Kausch was born in Jädersdorf on March 3, 1911. In June 1933 he joined the *SS* as number 82 578. Serving at first with the *Leibstandarte* of the *SS*, he attended the *SS Junker* School in Braunschweig from April 1935 to January 1936. In the *SS Totenkopf-Standarte* 1 "Oberbayern" he served as company chief, and took part in the western campaign as Commander of the 5th Battery of the *SS Totenkopf* Artillery Regiment. There he was awarded both Iron Crosses in August 1940. In November of that year he became Division Adjutant of the *SS* "Wiking" Division, and in August 1941 he took over the 1st Battalion of the Artillery Regiment there. Retrained at an army school for leaders of armored battalions in Paris, Kausch received the command of the newly formed *SS*

Armored Battalion "Hermann von Salza." Promoted to *SS Obersturmbannführer* on June 21, 1944, he was awarded the Knight's Cross on August 23, 1944. In February 1945 he led the *SS* Armored Regiment 11, and on 23 April he was decorated with the Oak Leaves. Taken prisoner by the Soviets on 2 May, he returned to his German home on January 16, 1956.

Fritz Knöchlein was born in Munich on May 27, 1911, and joined the *SS* as number 87881. Serving in the *SS Totenkopf* units, he was Chief of the 3/.*SS Totenkopf* Infantry Regiment in 1940. On May 27, 1940, he had eight British soldiers shot as revenge for the shooting of two German prisoners of war. In the summer of 1942 he served in the *SS Totenkopf* Infantry Regiment 3, and there he led the 1st Battalion as an *SS Sturmbannführer* in 1943. In the new formation of the 16th *SS* Armored Grenadier Division "*Reichsführer-SS*" he was transferred from the 3rd *SS* Armored Division at the end of 1943 and named Commander of the II./*SS* Armored Grenadier Regiment 36. On March 13, 1944, he took over the *SS* Armored Grenadier Regiment 23 "Norge" after its Commander, *SS Obersturmbannführer* Arnold Stoffers, was killed on February 25, 1944. As of February 10, 1945, Knöchlein led the *SS* Volunteer Armored Grenadier Regiment 49. Decorated with the Knight's Cross to the Iron Cross on November 16, 1944 (*SS Obersturmbannführer* as of March 8, 1944), Knöchlein was sentenced to death by a British war court on October 25, 1948, and hanged on January 21, 1949.

Günther Krappe was born in Schilde on April 13, 1893, and entered military service as a *Fahnenjunker* on September 26, 1912. On March 12, 1914, he was promoted to Lieutenant in Fusilier Regiment 34. After World War I and his time in the *Reichswehr*, Krappe, promoted to Lieutenant Colonel on August 1, 1936, took command of the III./Infantry Regiment 73. His promotion to Colonel was announced on April 1, 1939. Krappe served as a military attaché in Budapest, and later in Madrid. With his promotion to Major General on November 1, 1942, he took part in a division leader training course and commanded the 61st Infantry Division from February 1, 1942, to December 15, 1944. On October 1, 1943, he was promoted to Lieutenant General. In January 1945 he took part in a course for commanding generals, and as of February 10, 1945, he led the X. *SS* Army Corps. Krappe was decorated with the Knight's Cross to the Iron Cross.

Walther Krause was born in Schweidnitz on December 31, 1890, and entered military service on January 13, 1909. On June 16, 1910, he was commissioned a lieutenant in Infantry Regiment 156. After World War I Krause served in the *Reichswehr* and commanded as a colonel (January 1, 1938) Infantry Regiment 96. After various brief services, he was promoted to Major General on January 1, 1942, and as of October 1, 1942, commanded the 14th Infantry Division, then the 170th Infantry Division as of February 15, 1943. On July 15, 1944, Krause took over Division 462, and was promoted to Lieutenant General on 1 September of that year. As of October 15, 1944, the General, decorated with the Knight's Cross, was *Korück* of the 6th Army.

Walter Krüger was born in Strassburg, Alsace, on February 27, 1890, and served as a lieutenant in Grenadier Regiment 110 in 1908. In World War I he was decorated with the Iron Cross I and II among others, and he left the army as a captain in 1920, becoming a banker. In 1930 he moved to Carinthia, where he joined the banned SA in December 1933. In 1934 Krüger returned to Germany and worked under the Chief of Training of the SA. As of April 30, 1935, he commanded, as an *SS Obersturmbannführer*, the II./*SS Standarte* "Germania." After completing a course for regimental commanders, Krüger was promoted to *SS Standartenführer* on November 30, 1938, and on January 1, 1940, to *SS Oberführer*. With this rank he served first as 1st General Staff Officer and later as Leader of the *SS* Police Division. On December 13, 1941, decorated with the Knight's Cross to the Iron Cross, *SS Brigadeführer* and Major General of the *Waffen-SS* (promoted on April 20, 1941), Krüger became Inspector of the Infantry in the SS-FHA. On April 3, 1943—*SS Gruppenführer* and Lieutenant General of the *Waffen-SS* since January 30, 1942—he took over the 2nd *SS* Armored Division "Das Reich" and earned the Oak Leaves to the Knight's Cross on August 31, 1943. On January 25, 1944, Krüger was transferred to the Leader Reserve of the SS-FHA, and on 15 March of that year he became the Commander of the *Waffen-SS* "Ostland." After his promotion to *Obergruppenführer* and General of the *Waffen-SS* on June 21, 1944, he took command on July 15, 1944, of the VI. Weapon Army Corps of the *SS* (Latvian). Decorated with the Swords on January 11, 1945, Krüger took his life in Courland on May 22, 1945.

Dr. Gustav Krukenberg was born in Bonn on March 8, 1888. He took part in World War I as an active officer, finally as a captain in General Command, LVIII. Army Corps, and studied law and statecraft. Krukenberg joined the *SS* with number 116,685, and on January 30, 1938, he was named *SS Obersturmführer*. On December 1, 1943, he attained the rank of *SS Obersturmbannführer* and was transferred to *SS* Armored Grenadier Training and Replacement Battalion I. On January 17, 1944, he was promoted to Chief of General Staff V, *SS* Mountain Corps. On May 9, 1944, Krukenberg already became an *SS Oberführer* and Chief of the General Staff, VI. *SS* Volunteer Army Corps. Brief service positions followed; for example, as of September 1, 1944, he commanded the *Waffen-SS* "Ostland," and four weeks later became Inspector of the French *SS* volunteer units. On November 9, 1944,

Krukenberg was promoted to *SS Brigadeführer* and Major General of the *Waffen-SS*. In February 1945 he took over the 33rd *Waffen* Grenadier Division of the *SS* "Charlemagne" (French No. 1), and finally, on April 25, 1945, he replaced *SS Brigadeführer* and Major General of the *Waffen-SS* Ziegler as Commander of the 11th *SS* Volunteer Armored Grenadier Division "Nordland."

Christian-Peter Kryssing was born in Kolding, Denmark, on July 7, 1891. He became a career officer, and was promoted to captain on April 1, 1927. As Commander of the 5th Artillery Battalion, Kryssing was promoted to Lieutenant Colonel on November 1, 1937. Chosen by the Danish side as Commander of the Volunteer Unit "Dänemark," there was growing unrest, because of his strictly apolitical position, in the Danmark Free Corps, as it was named in August 1941. The result was the transfer of Legion *Obersturmbannführer* Kryssing at first to the *SS Totenkopf* Division and, from July 31, 1942, to April 2, 1943, to the *SS* Armored Grenadier Division "Wiking." Promoted to *SS Standartenführer* on January 30, 1943, he was as first supposed to lead the Armored Battalion in the *SS* Armored Grenadier Division "Nordland," but was then—after his promotion to *SS Brigadeführer* on August 1, 1943 (on 20 April he was briefly named an *SS Oberführer*)—the Artillery Leader of the III. (Germanic) *SS* Armored Corps. North of Narva he led the "Küste" Battle Group in the spring of 1944, which was then 9000 men strong. In 1945 he returned to Denmark and was there sentenced to five years in prison. Kryssing died in Haldersleben (North Schleswig) on July 7, 1976.

Jonas Lie was born in Norway on December 31, 1899, and studied law. In 1930 he joined the police and, four years later, the National Assembly. In 1939 he was called into the Norwegian Army as a captain. After the German occupation of Norway in the spring of 1940, Lie held various posts in the police and finally became Police Minister. In 1941, with number 401,276, he joined the *SS* and formed the Norwegian (General) *SS*. As an *SS Hauptsturmführer* (as of February 28, 1943, *SS Sturmbannführer* d.R.), Lie led a Norwegian police company from September 1942 to April 1943. An opponent of Quisling, the *Führer* of the NS in Norway, Lie died in prison after the war.

Erich von Lewinski, named von Manstein, was born in Berlin on November 24, 1887. He entered the 3rd Foot Guard Regiment and attended the War Academy in 1913-14. In World War I, von Manstein was finally the 1st General Staff Officer of the 213th Infantry Division, and then he went into the *Reichswehr*. In February 1934 he worked as Chief of Staff of Defense Zone III in Berlin and, in February 1938, took command of the 18th Division in Liegnitz. In the mobilization of 1939 he became Chief of the General Staff of

Army Group "South," and in October 1939 of Army Group A. Then he was named to lead the XXXVIII. Army Corps, and was awarded the Knight's Cross in 1940. In March 1941 he took over the LVI. Armored Corps—half a year later he was named Commander of the 11th Army. After the conquest of Sevastopol he was promoted to Field Marshal. With this rank he commanded Army Group "Don"—later "South" as of November 1942. At the end of March 1944 Hitler relieved Manstein, meanwhile decorated with Oak Leaves and Swords, of his post. He did not serve anymore in World War II.

Hasso von Manteuffel was born in Potsdam on January 14, 1897, and entered military service as a *Fähnrich* on February 22, 1916. He took part in World War I and was a member of the *Reichswehr*, and on February 1, 1939, he became a teacher at the Armored Troop School. As of June 13, 1940, he led Motorcycle Rifle Battalion 3, and then the I./ Rifle Regiment 7. Then came Armored Grenadier Regiment 6 as of August 25, 1941, as whose commander he was promoted to colonel on October 1, 1941. From July 15 to November 4, 1942, Manteuffel commanded the 7th Armored Grenadier Brigade, and as of February 8, 1943, the "Manteuffel" Division. After his promotion to Major General on May 1, 1943, he took over the 7th Armored Division, and on February 1, 1944, he was promoted to Lieutenant General and put in command of the "Grossdeutschland" Armored Division. Again simultaneously with a promotion—this time to General of the Armored Troops—on September 1, 1944, he was given a new task: the command of the 5th Armored Army. On March 5, 1945, having been decorated with the Knight's Cross, Oak Leaves, Swords, and Diamonds, he took command of the 3rd Armored Army.

Ernst Michael was born in Weimar on April 28, 1897, and joined the military as a *Fahnenjunker* on June 18, 1915. On July 14, 1916, he was made a lieutenant in Engineer Battalion 5. After World War 1 and the *Reichswehr* era he was an instructor at the War School in Hannover as of October 1935. Promoted to Lieutenant Colonel on December 1, 1939, he led the 1./Infantry Regiment 43 as of February 18, 1940. On June 1, 1941, Michael received the rank of Colonel and led Infantry Regiment 2 until April 28, 1943. In May 1943 he took part in division leader training and took over the 205th Infantry Division in May 1943. From November 25, 1943, to his death on January 22, 1944, he commanded the 9th *Luftwaffe* Field Division. Michael had received the German Cross in Gold and the Knight's Cross.

Anton Adriaan Mussert was born in Werkendam, North Brabant, Netherlands, on May 11, 1894, and, along with Cornelis Van Geelkerken, formed the "National Socialist Movement" (NSB) on December 14, 1931. In 1935 Mussert achieved his first small success in an election, but could not come to power. Only with the German occupation of Holland in May 1940 did he receive from Hitler an influential position as a collaborator. On 11 September of that year Mussert founded the "Nederlandsche SS" as a branch of the NSB, and at the end of 1940 he swore a personal oath to Hitler as *Führer* of the Great Germanic *Reich*. In 1943, though he had little support from his own people, he took the grandiose title of "Leider van het Nederlandse volk" ("Leader of the Netherlands People"). For his cooperation with Germany and, among other things, the deportation of Jewish people from Holland, Mussert was executed on May 7, 1946.

Vidkun Quisling was born in Fyresdal, Norway, on July 18, 1887, and joined the Royal Norwegian Army in 1911. In 1918-19 he functioned as Military Attache in St. Petersburg, and until his departure from active service in 1921 he was Military Attache in Finland. In the following years he worked for the release of German, Austrian, and Hungarian prisoners of war from the Soviet Union. From 1931 to 1933 he was the Norwegian Defense Minister, and on May 17, 1933, he founded the right-oriented "Nasjonal Samling" Party. When the German *Wehrmacht* occupied Norway in April 1940, Quisling hoped to be able to taker power. But since he had no support from the Norwegian people Hitler refused him. Only when the Norwegian resistance strengthened did Hitler install him as Norwegian Prime Minister on February 1, 1942. He served until 1945; because of his collaboration with Germany, Quisling was executed on October 24, 1945.

Wilhelm Rediess was born in Heinsberg on October 10, 1900. After training as an electrician, he was drafted in 1918, but did not reach the front. From 1919 to 1924 he worked for a farmer, after which he took various jobs. In 1925 Rediess joined the NSDAP and the SA with number 25 574, and in 1929 the *SS* with number 2 839. In 1932 he took part in the murder of a KPD member in Königsberg, and a year later he was a member of the *Reichstag*. On March 15, 1934, he was promoted to *SS Brigadeführer*, and to *SS Gruppenführer* a year later. From 1936 to June 19, 1940, Rediess worked as *Oberabschnittsführer* "Nordost," then as a high *SS* and Police Leader "Nord." In this position he was named *SS Gruppenführer* and Lieutenant General of the Police on April 9, 1941. Promoted to *SS Obergruppenführer* and General of the police in the autumn of 1941, Rediess was also named General of the *Waffen-SS*. He committed suicide in Oslo on May 8, 1945.

Fritz von Scholz was born in Pilsen, Bohemia, on December 9, 1896. He took part in World War I in the imperial and Royal Army, becoming a first lieutenant. Then he fought in the Oberland Free Corps in Upper Silesia in 1921. Afterward he worked as a chemical engineer, and was active in the NSDAP in Austria. Emigrating from the later

Ostmark in 1933, he joined the *SS Verfügungstruppe* on June 10, 1933, and as of August 17, 1938, he led the II./*SS Standarte* "Der Führer" as an *SS Sturmbannführer* since April 1, 1938. Promoted to *SS Obersturmbannführer* on January 30, 1940, he became an *SS Standartenführer* a year later. As of October 1, 1941, Scholz commanded the "Nordland" (mot.) Regiment. On January 18, 1942, Scholz was awarded the Knight's Cross to the Iron Cross, and on December 21, 1942, he was promoted to *SS Brigadeführer* and Major General of the *Waffen-SS*. For a short time he led the 2nd *SS* Infantry Brigade (mot.), and as of May 1, 1943, he took over the *SS* Armored Grenadier Division "Nordland." On March 12, 1944, Scholz was decorated with the Oak Leaves to the Knight's Cross, and on April 20, 1944, he was named *SS Gruppenführer* and Lieutenant General of the *Waffen-SS*. He fell on the Narva front on July 28, 1944, and on 8 August of that year he was posthumously awarded the Swords to the Oak Leaves to the Knight's Cross.

Hyazinth Graf Strachwitz von Gross Zauche und Camminetz was born in Gross Stein, Upper Silesia, on July 30, 1893. In the summer of 1912 he began his military career, and on February 17, 1914, he was named Lieutenant in the "Garde du Corps" Regiment. After World War I he was discharged in 1921 and reactivated in 1935. He first served as Captain of Cavalry Regiment 7. As a Major, Count Strachwitz first led a company in Armored Regiment 2, and later the 1st Battalion. His promotion to Lieutenant Colonel (January 1, 1942) was followed a year later by the promotion to Colonel and the command of the "Grossdeutschland" Armored Regiment. Before being promoted to Major General on April 1, 1944, he commanded an armored group in Army Group "North." In the summer of 1944 he commanded an armored unit to relieve Tukkums and Riga. Effective June 8, 1944, Count Strachwitz took over the Armored Instructional Division, and on January 1, 1945, he was promoted to Lieutenant General and became Commander of the Armored Divisions and Jagdverbände in Silesia. The General, decorated with the Oak Leaves, Swords, and Diamonds to the Knight's Cross, was then a reserve officer.

Martin Unrein was born in Weimar on January 1, 1901, and joined Infantry Regiment 71 as a *Fähnrich* on March 18, 1918. Taken into the *Reichswehr*, he was promoted to Lieutenant in Cavalry Regiment 9 on July 1, 1922. As a Major he was Adjutant of the XI. Army Corps. On January 15, 1940, Unrein took over Reconnaissance Battalion 268, and was named Lieutenant Colonel on 1 December of that year. As of September 15, 1941, he commanded Motorcycle Battalion 6, and as of April 1, 1942, Armored Grenadier Regiment 4. Three months later Unrein was promoted to Colonel. On November 5, 1943, he took command of the 14th Armored Division, which fought later in Courland. Unrein was promoted to Major General and Lieutenant General on January 1 and July 1, 1944. On February 11, 1945, bearing the German Cross in Gold and the Knight's Cross with Oak Leaves, he took command of the III. (Germanic) *SS* Armored Corps in Pomerania.

Bodo von Wartenberg was born in Luggendorf on December 6, 1890, and joined the army as a *Fahnenjunker* on October 22, 1910. On June 19, 1912, he was named a lieutenant in Guard Grenadier Regiment 2. After taking part in World War I, Wartenberg served in the *Reichsheer*. As a colonel he commanded Infantry Regiment 196 when the war began, and as of February 1, 1940, he became commander of a weapon school in Defense Zone III. He then served in Infantry Replacement Regiment 3 and Replacement Brigade "Grossdeutschland." On January 1, 1943, he was named Major General and named Commander of East Troops z.b.V. 703. As of October 16, 1943, he held the position of Commander of East Troops in the O.B. "West," and as of May 22, 1944, the title of Commander of Volunteer Troops in O.B. "West." On July 8, 1944, he took over the position of Commander of Volunteer Units with the Commander of the Replacement Army, and as of September 9, 1944, he commanded the Volunteer Cadre Division. Wartenberg died in Bad Honnef in 1954.

Hermann von Wedel was born in Magdeburg on July 27, 1893, and entered the military as a *Fahnenjunker* in 1911. On November 19, 1912, he was named a lieutenant in Grenadier Regiment 8, and after taking part in World War I he was discharged from active service. On October 1, 1935, Wedel was transferred from police service to the *Wehrmacht* as a captain and named Commander of the I./Infantry Regiment 80. He led it—promoted to Major on December 1, 1939, and Lieutenant Colonel on December 1, 1939—until 1942. Then he took over Infantry Regiment 590, and after being promoted to Major General (June 1, 1943) he commanded the 10th *Luftwaffe* Field Division. On January 29, 1944, he was wounded and, decorated with the German Cross in Gold and the Knight's Cross, Wedel died in the Dorpat hospital on February 3, 1944.

Helmuth Weidling was born in Haklberstadt on November 2, 1891, and entered the Imperial Army as a *Fahnenjunker* in 1911. After taking part in World War I and serving in the *Reichsheer*, he commanded, as a colonel (since March 1, 1938), Artillery Regiment 56 as of November 10, 1938, then Artillery Regiment 20 and Arko 128. Promoted to Major General, Weidling took over the 86th Infantry Division on January 1, 1942. He commanded the XXXI. Armored Corps—being promoted to Lieutenant General on January 1, 1943, and General of the Artillery on January 1, 1944—from October 20, 1943, to July 20, 1944. Then he took over the LVI. Armored Corps and was named Combat Commander of Berlin in April 1945. Weidling, decorated with the Knight's Cross with Oak Leaves and Swords, was taken prisoner by the Soviets on May 1, 1945, and died a prisoner.

Maximilian Wengler was born in Rosswein, Saxony, on January 14, 1890. He entered military service as a *Fahnenjunker* in 1909 and was named a lieutenant in Infantry Regiment 133 on August 15, 1910. In 1919, as Captain, he was discharged. Reactivated at the beginning of World War II, he became a company chief in an infantry Regiment. As a major he led a battalion as of 1940, and with his promotion to Lieutenant Colonel of the Reserve in 1942 he commanded Infantry Regiment 366. On October 6, 1942, Wengler was decorated with the Knight's Cross to the Iron Cross. His promotion to Colonel of the Reserve followed on December 1, 1942. On February 22, 1944, as Commander of the Wengler Group, he earned the Oak Leaves to the Knight's Cross, and took command of the 227th Infantry Division on July 22, 1944. Named Major General of the Reserve in 1945, he received the Swords to the Knight's Cross on 21 January of that year, and as of March 27, 1945, he led the 83rd Infantry Division. Wengler fell near Neutief, Pillau, on April 26, 1945.

Joachim Ziegler was born in Hanau on October 18, 1904, and, after graduating from school, joined the *Reichswehr* on April 1, 1923. For his participation in the Spanish Civil War he was decorated with the Cross of Spain. At the beginning of 1939 he was Captain and Adjutant in the 3rd Armored Brigade. On September 23, 1939, he was decorated with the Iron Cross II, and on June 28, 1940, with the Iron Cross I. On March 14, 1943, as a Colonel in the General Staff of the XXXXII. Army Corps, Ziegler received the German Cross in Gold. Transferred from the *Wehrmacht* to the *Waffen-SS* on June 1, 1943, he served as Chief of General Staff, III (Germanic) *SS* Armored Corps as of 20 June of that year. Effective November 9, 1943, he was named Commander of the *Waffen-SS* for the duration and allowd to wear the uniform of an *SS Oberführer*. As successor to the fallen *SS Gruppenführer* and Lieutenant General of the *Waffen-SS* von Schjolz, he took command of the 11th *SS* Volunteer Armored Grenadier Division "Nordland," and was taken into the *Waffen-SS* as *SS Brigadeführer* and Major General of the *Waffen-SS* on August 1, 1944. On September 5, 1944, Ziegler was awarded the Knight's Cross to the Iron Cross, and in mid-April 1945 he earned the Oak Leaves. Because of his independence in leading the 11th *SS* Volunteer Armored Grenadier Division "Nordland," he was removed as Division Commander on April 25, 1945, and was no longer awarded the Oak Leaves. Ziegler fell in the Humboldthain area of Berlin in the fighting to break out of Berlin on May 2, 1945.

Appendix 10

Waffen-SS and Army Ranks as of 1944

SS-Grenadier	*Waffen-Grenadier*[111]	*Grenadier*
SS-Sturmmann	*Waffen-Sturmmann*	*Gefreiter*
SS-Rottenführer	*Waffen-Rottenführer*	*Obergefreiter*
SS-Unterscharführer	*Waffen-Unterscharführer*	*Unteroffizier*
SS-Scharführer	*Waffen-Scharführer*	*Unterfeldwebel*
SS-Oberscharführer	*Waffen-Oberscharführer*	*Feldwebel*
SS-Hauptscharführer	*Waffen-Hauptscharführer*	*Oberfeldwebel*
SS-Untersturmführer	*Waffen-Untersturmführer*	*Leutnant*
SS-Obersturmführer	*Waffen-Obersturmführer*	*Oberleutnant*
SS-Hauptsturmführer	*Waffen-Hauptsturmführer*	*Hauptmann*
SS-Sturmbannführer	*Waffen-Sturmbannführer*	*Major*
SS-Obersturmbannführer	*Waffen-Obersturmbannführer*	*Oberstleutnant*
SS-Standartenführer	*Waffen-Standartenführer*	*Oberst*
SS-Oberführer	*Wafen-Oberführer*	no comparable rank
SS-Brigadeführer	*Waffen-Brigadeführer*	*Generalmajor*
SS-Gruppenführer	*Waffen-Gruppenführer*	*Generalleutnant*
SS-Obergruppenführer	*Waffen-Obergruppenführer*	*General*
SS-Oberstgruppenführer	*Generaloberst*	

111. Foreign soldiers who served in armed *Waffen-SS* units bore the prefix "Waffen-" to their rank instead of "SS-" or "Volunteer" as of June 1944.

Index of Names

Bibliography

Birn, Ruth, *Die Höheren SS- und Polizeiführer*, Tuebingen 1985
Friessner, Hans, *Verratene Schlachten*, Hamburg 1956
Haupt, Werner, *Die Heeresgruppe Mitte*, Dorheim 1968
———, *Die Heeresgruppe Nord*, Bad Nauheim 1966
Heiber, Helmut, ed., *Legebesprechungen im Führerhauptquartier*, Munich 1964
Klietmann, Dr. K.-G/, *Die Waffen-SS*, Osnabrueck 1965
Krätschmer, E.-Günther, *Die Rittergreuzträger der Waffen-SS*, Pr. Oldendorf 1982
Lindenblatt, Helmut, *Pommern 1945*, Leer 1993
Meissner, Gustav, *Dänemark unterm Hakenkreuz*, Frankfurt am Main 1990
Michaelis, Rolf, *Esten in der Waffen-SS*, Berlin 2000
———, *Die Panzer-Grenadier-Divisionen der Waffen-SS*, Berlin 1998[2]
Miehe, Walter, *Der Weg der 225. Infanterie-Division*, Hamburg 1980
Mörke, Fritz, *Der Kampf um den Kreis Arnswalde im Jahr 1945*, Göttingen 1984
Neulen, Hans Werner, *An deutscher Seite*, Munich 1985
Paul, Wolfgang, *Der Endkampf um Deutschland*, Esslingen 1976
Poller, Herbert, *Unsere Ehre heist Treue*, Bayreuth 1991
Preardovich, Nikolaus von, *Die Generaele der Waffen-SS*, Berg 1985
Scheibert, *Horst, Die Träger des Deutschen Kreuzes in Gold/Silber*, Friedberg, no year
Schramm, Percy, ed., *Kriegstagebuch der OKW 1940-1941*, Munich 1982
Seemen, Gerhard von, *Die Ritterkreuzträger*, Friedberg 1976
Steiner, Felix, *Die Freiwilligen*, Rosenheim 1992[7]
Tieke, Wolfgang, *Tragödie um die Treue*, Coburg 1996
———, *Im Lufttransport an Brennpunkte der Ostfront*, Osnabrueck 1971
anonymous, *Die Wehrmachtberichte 1939-1945*, Munich 1985

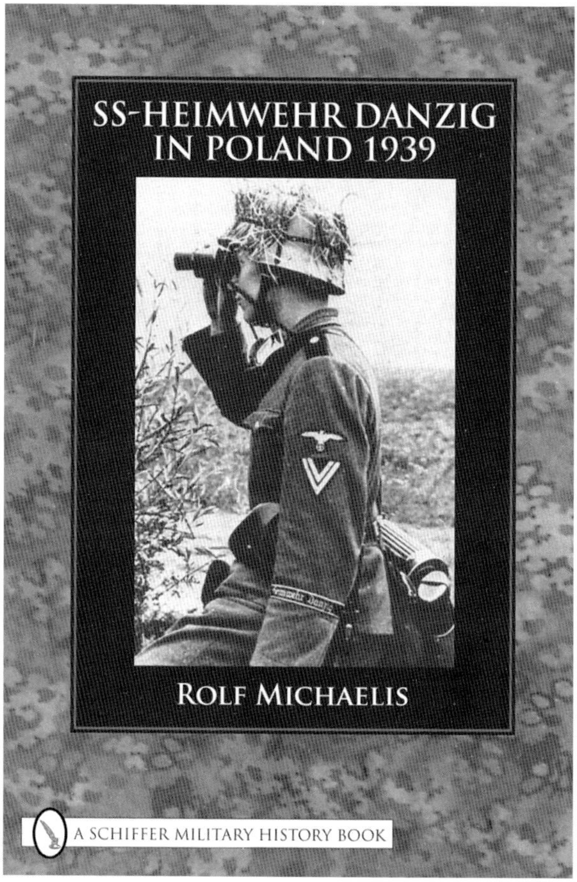

SS-Heimwehr Danzig in Poland 1939

Rolf Michaelis

This is the first book in English on this obscure early-World War II SS unit. In July 1939, SS-Heimwehr Danzig was formed from members of the III./4. SS-Totenkopf-Standarte "Ostmark," as well as from Danzig citizen volunteers. As a unit of the Reichsführer-SS they reinforced other existing Danzig units for the impending invasion of Poland. This book not only describes the political background that led to their deployment in September 1939, but also contains the combat recollections of former members, as well as over 100 photographs, and documents.

ISBN: 9780764329432, 6"x9", over 140 bw images
112 pp, hard cover, $29.95

SS-Fallschirmjäger-Bataillon 500/600

Rolf Michaelis

This book is the history of the only Fallschirmjäger-Bataillon of the Waffen-SS during World War II. Formed in 1943 as a Bewährungsverband for special missions (guerrilla operations in the Balkans) the unit was deployed at many focal points of heavy combat on the eastern and western fronts. Nearly destroyed at the Schwedt and Alt-Küstrinchen bridgeheads, the remainder pulled back to the west over Parchim at the end of April 1945 and entered U.S. captivity in May 1945. This is their story, including extremely rare photographs.

ISBN: 9780764329449, 6"x9", over 70 bw images
120 pp, hard cover, $29.95

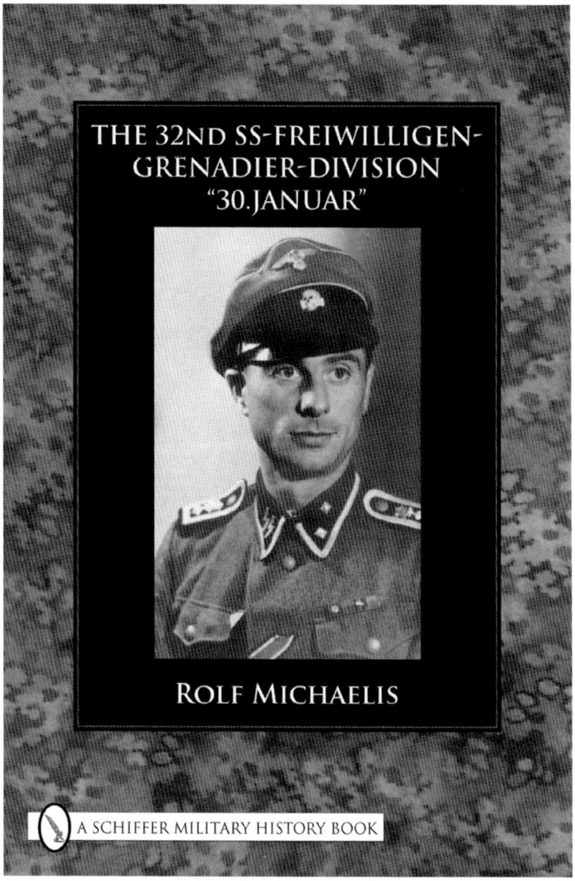

The 32nd SS-Freiwilligen-
Grenadier-Division
Rolf Michaelis

The SS Division "30. Januar" was one of the last SS-Divisions formed during World War II and was almost entirely composed of training units and 16-18 year old boys (the honorary name "30. Januar" was the same date Hitler became Reich chancellor in 1933). First planned as a motorized division, the unit ended up as a normal infantry division because of a lack of fuel. With a final strength of 12,000, they fought on the Oder-front south of Frankfurt/Oder. After the Soviet attack on 16 April 1945 they were wiped out in the pocket of Halbe southeast of Berlin.

ISBN: 9780764331015, 6" x 9", over 80 bw images
128 pp, hard cover, $35.00